What Parents Try to Forget about Adolescence

What Parents Try to Forget about Adolescence

Recall (if you dare) what it is like to be not quite an adult, not quite independent, and not quite sure of who you are.

Cliff Schimmels

LIFEJOURNEY
BOOKS

David C. Cook Publishing Co.
Elgin, Illinois   Weston, Ontario

LifeJourney Books is an imprint of David C. Cook Publishing Co.
David C. Cook Publishing Co., Elgin, Illinois 60120
David C. Cook Publishing Co., Weston, Ontario

WHAT PARENTS TRY TO FORGET ABOUT ADOLESCENCE
(Also published as *When Junior Highs Invade Your Home*)
© 1989 Cliff Schimmels

Cover design by Russ Peterson
Book design by April Frost
Back cover photo by Ron Ericksen Photography

First printing, 1989
Printed in the United States of America
93 92 91 90 89 5 4 3 2 1

Schimmels, Cliff.
        What Parents Try to Forget about Adolescence
        1. Junior high schools—United States. 2. Child rearing—
                United States. 3. Junior high school students—
                United States. 4. Adolescence   I. Title
        LB 1623.S35 1989
        373.73—dc19
ISBN   1-55513-151-4
                        89-760
                        CIP

CONTENTS

INTRODUCTION: WELCOME TO THE WONDERFUL WORLD OF JUNIOR HIGH

Junior High: A World of Extremes

H eidi was sick and missed the constitution test. In our school, that is a big deal. The constitution test is one of the biggest academic happenings of the year, one of those grade-level benchmarks that students encounter all through the schooling process.

People in first grade learn to read; people in third grade learn to write cursive; people in fifth grade learn to add fractions; and, in our state, people in eighth grade study the constitution and take a big test. The constitution test is one of those tasks assigned to a certain level of development. Few people ever study the constitution before the eighth grade—at least in our school.

But Heidi was sick and missed the test. The next day, we discussed a make-up time and agreed on Thursday afternoon right after school.

When the time came, I was ready with the make-up test all prepared. I don't forget things like that. I may not remember my wife's birthday, and I may walk home with the car still in the school parking lot, but I don't forget make-up tests.

Yet just as the bell rang to dismiss school, I got a note telling me to come downstairs for a telephone call. It was one of those calls from the district office; they were trying to arrange a committee meeting. I had to check my calendar for open dates. The other people checked their calendars. We shuffled and bargained. Finally, twenty minutes later, we came up with a date for the meeting, and I rushed back up to my classroom.

There sat Heidi, just about to boil over. I tried to explain and apologize, but nothing helped. Heidi's eruption came with me standing right in the middle of its wake.

Her mother was coming in *ten* minutes. She just *had* to go to town today to buy some new cheerleader shoes. There was a game tomorrow and the cheerleaders were going to wear uniforms all day. She had been there when I asked her to be. She had studied for the stupid old test the night before and worried about it all day long. She had better things to do with her time than sit in that stupid old room and wait for me to talk on the phone. Now she didn't have time to take that stupid old test. She just might *never* take it. She didn't care if she *did* flunk eighth grade. It was all my fault anyway. And no, she wasn't mad, and those weren't tears flowing down her cheek. And she was just going to leave, and there wasn't anything I could do about it.

She shut her books, got up, stormed out of

the room with the grace of a hippopotamus, and slammed the door. The sound jarred the tranquility of the then empty building—as well as my soul.

I guess I have been an adult too long to take such things as that in stride. I felt terrible about the incident. Not even the funniest rerun of "M*A*S*H" that evening could shake me loose from my concern. All night long I tossed and tumbled because I could not forget that girl in her misery.

Actually, I knew Heidi was right. We had made an agreement, and I had not kept my word. I should have been there. But how often am *I* kept waiting twenty minutes? I wait that long for a doctor's appointment. I wait that long to get in to see the principal, even when I have an urgent matter. And I don't respond that violently, even though I may feel like it.

I felt myself caught between being angry and being sympathetic about her hurt feelings. And underlying all that was my own sense of guilt, knowing that if I had been on time, none of it would have happened.

I didn't want to go back to school the next day. I had twenty good relationships with eighth graders, but that one bad one was enough to sour the whole day. I didn't know how to face Heidi, and I didn't know how Heidi would face me. I dreaded the tension that would permeate the atmosphere of the whole class. But, obedient to duty, I plodded back.

Before the beginning of the first period, I

stood outside the door to my room watching the half-children/half-adults scamper to class. (This is a common ritual for junior high teachers. We are instructed to watch out for students running in the hall, for boys punching boys they dislike and girls they *do* like, and for drug deals going down.) Just as I had lost myself in the activity of watching and had almost stopped dreading what was to come, a voice in the proximity of my right elbow said, "Mr. Schimmels?"

I turned and looked into that shining, beaming, sparkling face that belonged to Heidi.

"Mr. Schimmels," she said in tones dripping straight from the beehive, "are you mad at me?"

A World of Extremes

Welcome to the wonderful world of junior high, middle school, young adolescence, or whatever it is you call those frantic, fruitful, frightful years that engulf people between the ages of twelve and fifteen.

Theirs is a world of extremes—of emotions and moods, sizes and shapes, dreads and desires, aims and ambitions. These years represent one of the most exciting and trying spans of life, both for the people caught in the period and for the people who inherit the job of helping them through it.

Since you are reading this book, I assume you are one of the latter—someone with a special interest in helping a particular person through this period of extremes and adjustments. Perhaps you have a specific problem for which you need an answer, or perhaps you are just a bit frightened by the whole enterprise. Maybe you are just looking for confirmation of what you are already doing. Regardless of your motivation for reading it, I really want this book to help you.

If this were a typical how-to book, I would respond to your needs by developing a list of dependable generalities pertaining to junior-high age people and then making some specific suggestions about how you should respond to these general needs and moods. Then you could apply the salve to the sore, and we could all go away content that we had done our jobs.

But this isn't a typical how-to book, because we are not talking about *typical* people. There simply is no such animal as the "typical junior-high person." Each one is different, and each one changes every day. Every human being is the unique work of an omniscient God, who surely labors over each one of us until He gets us special. Yet during no period of life is human uniqueness more evident than during the junior high years. All the juices of life—emotions, moods, hungers, passions—come to the surface for the first time, and they come with such force that they shock and amaze the participants.

Let's face it. Junior high is a rough time. If you think it's rough for you as a parent, think for a moment about what the poor teenager is going through. Try to stumble a few steps in his Nikes or boat shoes.

And that leads me to the purpose of this

book. I have already told you that it is not a typical how-to book. There are simply too many extremes to be gathered up and grasped by a few generalities. Instead, I want to give you a glimpse of some specific junior-high people involved in the very acts of living—doing and feeling, acting and reacting.

These descriptive anecdotes have been gathered over many years and from many sources. I taught and coached junior high students for a lot of years, and I still visit junior high schools regularly. Many of my closest friends are presently dedicated, knowledgeable junior-high teachers. And, if I may boast, I just promoted the youngest of my own three children to the beautiful age of fifteen and the "high schooler" title that goes with it. As a parent, I am now an expert. In other words, I have a perspective with distance.

As you will see, many of these episodes do originate in school, and you will probably wonder why. My purpose is to help you understand—to help you get a glimpse of your junior higher in both natural and artificial settings. The school is a dominant force in the overall lives of these people.

If your child shows certain attitudes and behavior at school, he will probably carry those home with him—and to church and to scouts and to every area of his life.

As you read some of these vignettes, your first thought may be, *My junior higher isn't like that at all*. But keep reading—I may get to your child before I am finished. And who knows? Your child may evolve into one of these characters before God is finished with him or her.

For example, Heidi was normally a sweet, cooperative, popular young lady. So why did she forsake all her dignity and poise to make a point with a temper tantrum that she didn't even approve of herself? How could she react so violently—and heal so quickly?

Something to Count On

Assuming that temper tantrums are not normal behavior for Heidi and that she was not intentionally experimenting with a new method of manipulating adults, there had to be some cause for her behavior, which actually shocked both of us. My guess is that it was disappointment.

At this point in her development, Heidi's life is characterized by change and flux. There are very few things that are stable and dependable. Her friends are changing. One day they are short and cutesy fat; the next day they are tall and lean. One day they sing tenor; the next day they sing bass.

And Heidi herself is changing. When you are in junior high, looking into the mirror is like looking at the mountains. Every day you see something you have never seen before. Even though you may like what you see, you are still a little worried about how it will all work out in the end. One day you are beautiful; the next day you have a pimple on your nose. There is always some risk.

With changes in appearance come changes in personalities. Friendly people become sour; sour people become popular. Straight friends start stealing nips from Daddy's liquor cabinet, and they prod you to join them. You tell your best friend your latest secret crush, and the next day you catch her flirting with him. Promises are broken; dependable people can't be trusted, and you are constantly bracing yourself to expect the unexpected.

Heidi may not be conscious of all this, but it is there, and she can feel it even if she doesn't know it. Surely, Heidi is entitled to *something* dependable and constant and consistent. What shall she choose? Teacher! It has a ring of promise to it. Most teachers she has met have been fairly nice. Why, the position itself means authority and respect; she's been taught that all her life. So when I didn't show for our appointment, I not only forsook her trust, but I undermined her source of consistency. I became just another undependable nuisance she would have to tolerate.

Heidi wanted authority and consistency. When I didn't deliver, she tried to get back at my inconsistency by doing something inconsistent herself. It was more than an attack on me. It was a statement of her disappointment.

If ours had been a daughter-parent relationship and I had committed such a breach of her expectation, Heidi would still have had to react.

One common way to do so is to run away from home.

In recent years, I have asked hundreds of well-adjusted college students if they ever ran away from home. About 30 percent sheepishly hang their heads, study their shoe shine with feigned intensity, clear their throats several times, then quietly relate an experience when, in total frustration, they summoned up as much courage as they could find, packed a small bag, and left home forever. Of course, most were back in a matter of hours, and the event now lies only in their memories as a source of embarrassment.

The explanation for this now regrettable behavior is almost always the same—the dependability of the adult world broke down. These young people had to lash out against the perceived injustice, and this was the most serious form of rebellion they could think of. As parents and teachers, we should take great care not to needlessly let down our junior high children. At their age, they might quickly find a more serious way to rebel. We should strive to always be there when they expect us—even when important phone calls threaten to pull us away.

Homework Assignments for Parents

1. How dependable would your junior higher say you are? When you say you'll do something, do you *always* come through? In what other ways can you convince your child that you'll always be there for him?

2. How is your junior higher like all the others you know in his age-group? In what ways is he different? Which of his distinctives do you most appreciate?

What We Try So Hard to Forget

R ecently I attended one of those after-church parties of about five couples. The conversation turned to good times—especially stories about growing up. We grew increasingly loud and bold as we laughed at our youthful foibles, and I decided to take the opportunity to do some research for this book. I said, "I'll tell you what let's do. Let's all remember one fun story about when we were in junior high."

Immediately, stillness gripped the room. Sheets of it blanketed the group. Laughter turned to silence. Dancing eyes stopped in their joy. Meditation marked the brows.

Well, there are two things teachers can't stand—noise and silence. So I decided I would make the exam a little easier. "Let's just remember one thing that happened to us, good or bad, when we were in junior high."

That got the same response. Silently, people started getting up and leaving. I think the hostess is still upset with me for breaking up the party.

The people at the party were from diverse geographic locations—including Canada, the Southeast, the Midwest, and the East—so they must have been expressing a universal feeling. From my little bit of research, I concluded that most of us adults choose not to remember our junior high experience. We have simply stuffed those years way down deep in the memory box, hoping they never torment us again.

But now, holding the divinely ordained office of Parenthood, we find ourselves having to help our own children struggle through the period that we are trying to forget. Perhaps when they need us the most, we are the least prepared to identify with what is happening to them.

Yet being unprepared is no excuse to avoid the problem. While no one has all the answers in this complicated area, parents will benefit greatly if they have the discipline to consider and discuss some of the basic things they can do to help their junior highers. Here are a few suggestions to get you started.

Be consistent.

"**O**kay," you say, "I have heard that piece of advice so many times it is just another cliché. Tell me something new and pertinent."

But I'm serious. If you are the kind of parent concerned enough to read books to help you in your task, you have already made a great effort to be consistent, and your child and I thank you. But now the challenge is even greater. As consistency becomes more critical to your child, it also becomes harder to maintain. As life gets more complex, the arbitrary lines of decisions grow grayer. It is not going to be as easy as it has previously been to say yes or no.

When your child was younger, consistency was a matter of remembering what you said and keeping your word. But as your child grows into a new level of awareness and perception, and as he or she begins to observe subtleties of behavior and intentions, you have to back your word up with something more. Consistency now means living what you say.

I encourage you and your spouse to spend some time together making sure that the home front is unified. You could take a weekend off, go somewhere together, and talk until you have reached an agreement about how the two of you are going to react to some of the issues your junior higher will thrust upon you during the next few years. Let me suggest some topics worthy of such attention.

Dating

How early and how intense? Which of you is going to explain the facts of life and when? How deep are you going to go into that explanation? What will you do if you don't approve of your child's selection of dates?

Curfew

Not only do you need to agree on the hours, but you need to agree on the consequences when the curfew is broken. "Breathes there a teenager with soul so dead who never to himself has said, *Aw shucks, I can be late because my parents are already in bed?"*

Friends

Whom do you like? Are you going to interfere in the your child's selection of friends (subtly, of course)? Do you plan to emphasize church activities over other social possibilities? How are you going to handle it when your child makes a bad friend choice?

Grades

What are your expectations? Are they realistic? How are you going to react if your expectations are not met?

Activities

Will you insist on participation in extra-curricular events? How are you going to support your child's participation when he becomes involved?

Dress and appearance

What kinds of standards are you going to set? Who has the responsibility to enforce them?

Drugs and alcohol

Who is responsible for the instruction? How are you going to react if you discover that your child is experimenting?

Church activities

How much involvement are you going to insist on? Are you going to request (or demand) that the junior higher sit with the family during services?

Temper tantrums

Do you punish, panic, or ignore? What other forms of rebellion does your child tend to demonstrate?

Parental roles

Most children tend to talk to one parent about certain areas of their lives and to the other about different areas. Are you and your spouse aware of your individual roles, and are you comfortable with them?

This list could, of course, be much longer. But if you have at least agreed on a few things, you will probably find yourself compatible on other issues as they happen. The important thing is that your junior higher receives a model of consistency and stability from his parents.

Make no promises you can't keep.

This is probably just a repetition of the first point, but I am not afraid of being repetitive. The point is worth learning.

I am sure you are not the kind of parent who intentionally lies to your child, but during his junior high years it is important that you carry out all promises. If you promise to go to a hockey game on Thursday, you should take him to the hockey game on Thursday. If you say you're going to ground him if he breaks curfew, you should ground him if he breaks curfew.

Analyze your life for stressful changes.

In recent years we have read some strong warnings about stress-producing changes in an adult's life. We have learned to be cautious about our mental and physical health during such times as retirement, divorce, surrendering the last child to adulthood, unemployment, moving, or changing jobs. At the same time we should recognize that children also undergo stress during times of change, particularly during this period when the child's life is characterized by change.

If you have a junior-high-age child, you may very well be looking at some significant changes in your own life. This may be the time when you are thinking about moving out of your starter home to something more permanent. You may be considering a promotion that would drastically (or even slightly) alter your life-style. Your relationship with your spouse may be growing in one direction or another.

Of course, you can't avoid these changes. In many cases you wouldn't want to. But I do hope you realize that these stress-producing situations also cause stress in your children, particularly when they are at a stage when their whole world is changing.

Don't close doors behind your junior higher.

As I described in the last chapter, when I didn't show for my appointment with Heidi, she reacted with a rather unusual type of behavior. She was angry at the time, and her feeling for me was one of hatred. That may sound a bit strong, but I really think she hated me at the time. It was an honest emotion that came with the moment, and she had to try it on to see how it fit.

By the next morning, she had realized that hatred wasn't appropriate. At least, it wasn't the way she wanted to feel about me; so then she was faced with a new challenge. She had to glue her courage to the sticking place and try to come back into the relationship at a point where we had been before the hurricane hit. That took some real integrity and character on her part.

I suppose we could make a case for my demanding some act of penance from her. I had been wronged, at least partially. I could have threatened or at least demanded an apology, but I am not sure it was necessary. She had discovered on her own that her reaction was wrong. Through the incident, she had grown. What was important now was for me to accept her cheerfulness and her willingness to forget as apology enough.

Although it was probably by accident, I think I handled Heidi's situation correctly. I hadn't closed any doors behind her. She knew that when she was ready she could return and be welcomed.

This idea isn't original with me. I found it in Luke 15. When the prodigal son decided to come home after squandering all his inheritance, the father not only made it easy for him, he even threw a party.

We must keep our doors—and arms—open to our junior high sons and daughters, letting them know that there's *nothing* they can do that can make us stop loving them.

Homework Assignments for Parents

1. What are some of your fun stories from junior high? What are some of the painful ones? Have you told both sets of stories to your junior high child so he knows he's not alone in his confused feelings?

2. Are you prepared to help your junior higher face the changes that he will experience during the next several years? Have you talked through (or at least thought through) the issues suggested in this chapter?

SECTION 1: HELPING YOUR CHILD COPE WITH PHYSICAL CHANGES AND EMOTIONAL STRESS

Don't Judge a Junior Higher by Its Cover

C had and Kenneth were on the seventh-grade basketball team together. Kenneth was one of the most responsible thirteen-year-olds I have ever known. He kept his locker neat and orderly. He didn't have to hunt for his shoes or report one of his socks stolen (because he had really lost it). He took care of his equipment. He was always the first one out to practice.

Once on the practice floor, Kenneth did everything the coach asked. When the players ran laps, he always ran next to the wall and didn't cheat on the corners, even when the coach wasn't looking. When the coach blew his whistle, Kenneth immediately stopped dribbling and ran in to hear what the coach had to say.

Kenneth bought a stocking cap because Coach said to cover his head after practice. When Coach said to shoot with the left hand, Kenneth worked on it at home until he could do it. Not only did Kenneth know his own position, he also knew where every other player was supposed to be at all times. In short, Kenneth was a very responsible person and player.

On the other hand, one might have gotten the idea that Chad didn't care. He was late to practice almost every day, and he even skipped some times. Actually, he often had a good excuse because his teachers had kept him after school, but he still missed practice.

His locker was a shambles. His socks never matched. When lap time came, Chad loafed and cut corners. When Coach blew his whistle, Chad always took time to shoot another basket before he came in. He never listened when Coach talked—it was evident by the way he played. Chad never knew where he was supposed to be, so the coach had to hold up practice just to show him the correct position. In short, Chad was a very irresponsible person and player.

But I forgot to mention that Kenneth was four-six while Chad was an even six feet tall and well-developed for his age.

As the day of the first game approached, Kenneth became excited. A couple of days before, the coach had handed out uniforms. They might have looked like old eighth-grade hand-me-downs to you, but to Kenneth they were on par with what the Chicago Bulls wear. He didn't mind that he was the last person to get a uniform—at least he had one. After his mother tucked it in for him a bit, he hung it on his door so he could look at it and dream.

On the day of the game, Kenneth was the first one into the dressing room. He dressed quickly and waited for Coach to come and give that powerful speech before they went out on the floor. But when the coach got there, what he saw first was Chad—leaning against his locker, still in street clothes. Chad had forgotten his uniform.

Coach ranted and raved and talked of responsibility, while Chad hung his head and grinned. Finally, Coach devised a plan. Chad would just have to wear Kenneth's uniform, even if it looked ridiculous on him. Kenneth could sit on the bench and keep shot charts.

"Fiend!" you shout. "Foul! What a horrible man. How could he do such a despicable thing?"

But I ask you, if you were a young coach trying to win at the seventh-grade level in the hope of moving up to high school coaching, would you have let a six-foot giant sit on the bench on the small technicality that he had forgotten his uniform—while a four-foot-six kid who wasn't going to play in the game anyway was all suited up just to shoot around during warm-ups?

Size and Expectations

When do we teach people these hard, cruel facts of life? In fact, what did this young coach teach both boys (and the whole team) that day? That winning is the only thing that matters? That responsibility doesn't count for much? That life always favors the naturally gifted? Yet from your own experience, can you say that these lessons are all that false?

These are important questions which merit some serious consideration, but I just threw them in here to illustrate how often we unknowingly and unintentionally pass along our own values to junior highers. Their perceptions are probably keener than we think. I would like this incident to lie in the backs of our minds and haunt us a bit every time we make a quick decision or take an action affecting a learning, growing, changing young person.

Whether we agree with this coach's actions or not, we need to look at a couple of the basic factors at work here and see what we can learn from them.

The obvious difference between Kenneth and Chad was *size*. A foot and a half difference may be a little extreme; but size differences are common at this age. Not only are there differences between individuals, but any one person may encounter a serious size change in what seems like a matter of days.

Chad had probably grown six inches over the summer, and Kenneth would be likely to grow six inches the next summer. Pity the poor mothers and fathers who are trying to keep these guys in clothes, particularly if they are the kind of kids who are always concerned about how they look.

Adults can't do much about the contrast in size of junior highers. But we are able to control our *expectations* of the junior highers we know. Chad was big, but irresponsible. Kenneth was short, dependable, and unusually mature. Yet they were both thirteen years old. Imagine them side by side. Can you honestly say that you would be capable of treating them as equals? If the two of them showed up to do some yard work for you, could you pay them the same amount without any misgivings? Can you blame the coach for thinking that Kenneth wasn't "big enough" to care about the coach's decision?

This is one of the most serious challenges for people who live or work with junior highers: accepting the fact that a young person does not mature in all aspects of his character on the same schedule, and realizing that physical maturity is often deceptive.

Assessing Maturity

There is actually injustice here on both sides. In most people's eyes, Kenneth is still a child. Unless he develops physically, he will be treated as a child for the next two years. We give him the responsibility of a child and we expect him to act like a child, ignoring his potential and maturity.

Chad, on the other hand, is not only saddled with all that size, but is also burdened with people's greater expectations. They expect him to perform with more maturity than he actually has at this point. Age is no factor here. The bigger a person is, the more is expected of him.

Chad simply does not have the intellectual or emotional maturity to handle the adult responsibility demanded of him. He, like Kenneth, still has a natural need to punch, pester, choke, squeak, slouch, stumble, belch, drop, and forget.

He gets just as excited about a new hair on his chest and just as upset about a new pimple on his nose. Even if he has just scored twenty-five points in the basketball game, he still may trip over a line and fall on his face going back to the dressing room. At such times we need to remember that he is just another thirteen-year-old boy.

If you are going to be effective as a parent, you have to develop some method other than size and physical development to assess maturity. Thirteen-year-olds are thirteen years old regardless of how often they shave. This is one of the most difficult problems of the whole junior high scene. It is difficult for all the Chads and Kenneths (and Charlottes and Kristines), and it is difficult for the people who have to work with them.

Homework Assignments for Parents

1. Think about the size differences of the junior highers you know. Are you guilty of treating the larger ones more like adults than the smaller ones? If so, what things can you do in the future to treat all junior highers more equally?

2. How does your behavior reflect your values, even in ways you may not usually recognize? Can junior highers see that you are a fair person, or do your actions suggests certain prejudices and inequalities? What can you do to better correlate your actions with your intentions?

4

Good Looks, Bad Timing

I remember the first time I ever saw Jessica. I was eating lunch in the school cafeteria, discussing with some other junior high teachers such high-level issues as nuclear disarmament and why the Cowboys never win the Super Bowl. Suddenly, right in the midst of all this profoundness, the conversation stopped. I looked up from my food to see what had shocked us into a state of silence (an unusual condition even at the teacher's table in a junior high lunchroom), and I saw Jessica standing in line.

She was strikingly beautiful, and I began to fumble in my mind with who she might be—an especially mature high school student visiting our building, a student teacher from a nearby college, or perhaps a young mother. The principal, probably anticipating our questions, said, "That's Jessica, the new seventh grader who transferred here this morning."

We sat shocked. As junior high teachers, we had come to expect size and maturity differences in young people, but Jessica was the most extreme example we had ever seen.

As we became acquainted with her in class, we discovered that she had the personality, intelligence, and talent to match her beauty. She was simply a graceful person. Although she was not much sharper than the average seventh grader, she had a certain confidence about herself that carried over into her academic work. She also was cheerful and cooperative.

Because she was so mature physically, the other teachers and I expected her to be more mature in other ways. If she had not completed an assignment on time, we would have been more likely to accept her excuse than if she had looked like any other seventh grader. I don't tell an adult, "Eat your liver before you can have dessert," and I don't think I would have told that to Jessica either.

As the new kid on the block, Jessica was not as enthusiastically accepted by her classmates as she was by the teachers. The in-group (usually a well-established clique) didn't want her. She was too mature and too pretty. She would have had to come into the group as the leader, and the present leadership didn't want that. So she stayed outside.

The out-group is usually easier to get into. Since these people are a little lonely anyway, they welcome new members, so they adopted Jessica. But she didn't fit in there either.

At this point, she wasn't angry with the system. She was still worried about her studies and grades, and pleasing teachers and parents. Although she was gracious and bright enough not to offend anybody, she was never really comfortable with the people who were willing to accept her. Consequently, she spent her year in seventh grade being more popular with adults than with the people her own age. That was fine with the adults. We all enjoyed her friendship.

However, near the end of the year, Jessica revealed her true value system and made an emphatic statement about what she wanted in life. She wanted to be a typical, popular junior high girl—in other words, a cheerleader. She wanted to wave the pom-poms, chew bubble gum, and yell for the football team.

When tryouts came, she was one of the first to sign up. At our school, cheerleader tryouts were one of the major rites of the year. Each new, hopeful group tried with ever-increasing optimism to outdo everything that had ever been done before.

On the appointed day, the student body marched into the gym to the accompaniment of the band's playing the "Washington Post March." With giggling sincerity, the out-going captain made her farewell speech, a rousing plea for school spirit. Then, participating in pairs, the aspirants led the student body in a cheer as they demonstrated their talents at hollering and waving at the same time. Although Jessica looked a bit out of place because she was about a foot taller than her partner, she was, nevertheless, graceful through the whole ordeal. But when the students cast their secret ballots at the end of the ritual, Jessica didn't make it. She wasn't even close enough to be an alternate.

During the summer, I heard that Jessica was modeling for a local store. When school started the next fall, she was going steady with a high school junior who owned a nice car and a questionable reputation. After that, she only went through the motions of being in junior high. By the time she was seventeen, she had become actively involved in the drug culture, dropped out of school, and moved in with a man several years older than she was. I'm not sure where she is or what she is doing now.

When Beauty Comes Early

I realize that Jessica is a bit of an unusual case. She was not only mature, but also beautiful at thirteen. Yet she still represents a troublesome group—the junior high girls who mature physically before they do emotionally and intellectually. Jessica made a strong effort to fit into her own age-group, but at that point in a person's development, the age-group is rather narrowly defined. In adulthood, there isn't that much difference between the thirties and the fifties. In high schools, sophomores are frequently comfortable with seniors. But in the stage of early adolescence, seventh graders are seventh graders, and eighth graders are eighth graders.

When Jessica couldn't find her niche among her own age-group, she had to experiment and look outside. She knew she wasn't an adult, so she settled for the next step up—the high schoolers. Maybe she could find some companionship there.

As soon as she paid her dues into that group, she was suddenly thrust into decisions she wasn't prepared to make. Jessica was not experienced enough nor emotionally mature enough to make rational decisions about how to handle drugs or her own sexuality. But because of the way she looked, these decisions were forced on her at a time when peer acceptance was about her only basis for value judgments. It is difficult for anyone to try to live her life on the basis of what she thinks other people want her to do. Small wonder that Jessica became confused, disenchanted, and eventually hardened.

Jessica also teaches us another important lesson. Her story points out the vast difference between thirteen-year-olds and sixteen-year-olds. Sometimes those differences may not be immediately obvious. Thirteen-year-olds may look older, and they may even sound older. Some seventh graders can read, write, and talk as intelligently as many high school juniors. But those three to five extra years of studying at the University of Life have a tremendous value.

Jessica was a normal, sweet, girl who had the body of a woman. The people she encountered were more aware of (and more interested in) the woman than the girl. And we adults who should have know better unwittingly cheated her out of three critical years of development.

What could have been done to prevent Jessica's unhappiness and subsequent disillusionment? The answer to that is more difficult than I would like it to be. We could have told Jessica that being a cheerleader was not all that important, but I don't think she would have believed us. We could have tried to be closer to her ourselves, but she didn't want adult friendship. She already had that. What she wanted was to be a seventh grader among seventh graders. But it is not easy for parents or teachers to manipulate a group of seventh and eighth graders into accepting someone.

If you have a daughter who is maturing physically more rapidly than in other areas, I offer Jessica's story just as it stands. Your daughter may look like she is past this stage, but she is still a junior higher with all the trappings thereof. Your understanding, concern, and sensitivity are crucial.

When Beauty Fades Early

But what if you have just the opposite problem? What if your daughter's beauty fades earlier than all her friends'? In that case, consider Sara's example.

Sara's teacher was trying to help the seventh grade class understand the concept of romanticism—the idea that something in the distance looks good, but in reality isn't as much fun as you thought it was going to be. The concept was important to their understanding a short story about Southerners preparing for the Civil War.

To make the experience as personal as possible, the teacher asked, "Have any of you really looked forward to some event and then, when it came, you were totally disappointed by how it turned out?"

Sara's answer was terse and spontaneous. "Yeah. Junior high."

Sara wasn't just having a bad day. Her appraisal was accurate and permanent. So far, her seven months in junior high had been totally disappointing, and things weren't getting any better.

Sara had the flip side of Jessica's problem. Sara had been in school with many of her classmates since they started kindergarten. Very early, she had become a favorite of students and teachers alike. She was pretty and cheerful. She had a nice smile and a big heart. Her classmates loved and envied her at the same time.

She was a good student and had a quick wit, so with her combination of cute and neat, she was also the teacher's pet. But her classmates didn't resent her because she was so friendly.

As the students edged to the upper end of childhood and began to notice that the world was wonderfully coeducational in structure, Sara mastered the art of flirting. She spread her smiles over a wide enough area to accumulate several male interests, and at the same time she remained popular with the girls. Throughout elementary school, Sara was the center of attention.

But during the summer between sixth and seventh grades, when people are supposed to mature and change, a strange thing happened. Instead of growing tall and feminine as her friends did, Sara only added a few pounds to her already short stature (and in places not necessarily conducive to feminine charm).

When the students reconvened at the junior high in the fall to "ooh" and "aah" at how much everybody had changed over the summer, Sara soon began to lose her center-ring attraction. To make matters worse, she was replaced by her best friend. Although no one intended to be rude to Sara, it was just that the other girl suddenly looked like more fun, and people that age usually trust their eyes.

Sara had enough class not to make any scenes, but she quietly went about trying to reclaim some of the distinction she had lost. She became the first girl in class to wear eye makeup and, after intense pleading with her parents for two weeks, she got her ears pierced. Yet despite all her attempts at cosmetic improvement, things didn't change much. Her best friend was still the center of attention, both with the boys and the girls, and Sara was cast into a supporting role.

Such a change in status never comes easily, particularly when a person has enjoyed stardom as long as Sara had. And it was more painful because the change in roles was dictated by something as superficial as change in body style. Deep down inside, Sara was the same sweet, lovable person she had always been. But suddenly she didn't look as good as her friend on the outside. Why should she be penalized for that?

Sara's struggle, however, was real and deep and far too typical. Of course, it was tough on her, but Sara was a strong enough person to live through her junior high misery. She cried a lot; she was frequently sullen and moody; she spent a lot of time locked up in her room; and she bounced between hatred and loyalty for her classmates. But she survived.

In fact, by her junior year in high school she had managed to reclaim some of the popularity she had lost, and she finished high school on a rather positive note. Now that she is an adult, she has chosen to forget about junior high altogether, to block out of her mind all those unhappy memories of that period of transition.

What's a Parent to Do?

If Sara had been a little less strong, her change in roles could have been devastating. In fact, I chose Sara to illustrate this point because her story *does* end happily. None of us is happy when our children are unhappy, and any good parent will search for some remedy that will work. Unfortunately, Sara's parents were almost powerless to help. Her problem was something she had to go through alone.

So whether your child, like Jessica, matures early and has to endure the pressure that is involved, or is more like Sara, whose beauty (and popularity) came and went before entering junior high, here are a couple of suggestions to help you see her through those hard times:

First, if your child is nearing that age when body styles and appearance change rapidly, you may as well prepare yourself to suffer with her through some changes in social roles that come with the package. You can't speed up the transition or change the course of it, but you can provide some understanding and perhaps some diversion.

Second, perhaps the best help a parent can offer in similar situations is to help the junior higher see beyond the present. Of course, this is tough for any of us. But if life really becomes miserable for everybody, it might be worth a try. Spend some time with your child reflecting about what life is going to be. Talk of adult things such as work, marriage, and family. Give her some adultlike responsibility.

If you promise not to tell, I'll share my secret weapon, which I save for my children when they are struggling through these critical periods of reidentification. I find a vacant parking lot somewhere, and I teach them how to drive. You would be amazed at how much thirty minutes at the wheel in an isolated parking lot can do for a thirteen-year-old's morale!

It doesn't resolve the problem. They don't become any more socially accepted, although they may brag about their driving skills all over school. But they *have* been given a glimpse of what life is going to be like once they get past their immediate obstacles, and that seems to help.

Homework Assignments for Parents

1. Do you know any junior highers who, like Jessica, peaked early in the way they looked? Did you ever consider that this might actually be a negative experience for them? What can you do to help such junior highers "act their age"?

2. On the other hand, do you know any people like Sara, who are already losing popularity in junior high based solely on the way they look? How can you help combat the tendency junior highers have to judge by appearance only? Be specific in your answers.

Rejected!

T he teacher's instructions were given in all innocence: "Johnny, think of an adjective and use it in a sentence showing its three degrees."

But Johnny has been waiting all period for this opportunity. He quickly responds: "Robert is *fat*. Robert is *fatter* than anyone I have ever seen. Robert is the *fattest* person in the whole world."

"And the *laziest*," adds Charles.

"And the *ugliest*, yech!" adds Marie.

"You would be fat too if you ate like he does," adds another classmate.

Poor Robert . . . and this is still the first hour. Before the day is over, he will be kicked and punched, his sandwich will be squashed, someone will break his pencil, and he will be pushed off the sidewalk while trying to walk home with some of the guys.

Robert represents one of the most difficult challenges for a junior high teacher and even more so for a parent. Junior highers can be very understanding and loving—even tender, on rare occasions. But other times they can be brutally cruel, and usually their cruelty is directed toward one person—in this case, Robert.

Robert Serves a Purpose

I am not sure I know how Robert got the office of human football. In some ways he isn't quite as mature as the other students, but he is not *that* different. Sometimes he may not be so easy to be around, but many other students are just as capable of childish behavior. Yet for some reason, Robert has been designated as everyone else's morale booster. One of the ways to join the "in group" or prove oneself to be a thinking human being is to put Robert down. To achieve this end, almost anything is acceptable.

I don't know how Robert got "elected," but I do think I understand the need for the office. I don't approve, but I understand. It seems to me that there is an innate human need for each one of us to feel that we are better than someone else. This attitude may not be scripturally sound, but it seems to be fairly universal.

For the junior highers, this need seems to be particularly acute. Since they are in the process of change, they really don't know themselves very well. Many are at that awkward age of being too old to be cute and too young to be handsome or beautiful. They are beginning to identify some adult powers (such as reproduction), yet society tells them they shouldn't use these powers. In the midst of all these inconsistencies and contradictions, the junior highers need to reassure themselves that they are all right. They do so by suggesting that Robert *isn't*. (Adults seem to have the same need to feel superior, though their methods are usually more polite and sophisticated.)

What can we do for Robert? To a teacher, Robert presents an almost unsolvable problem. The English teacher could have stopped that in-class teasing. Had she been forceful enough, she could have made sure that it never occurred in English class again. But she could not have made Robert a popular hero, and the students would have just found another setting in which to persecute him. Besides, by punishing the students for their teasing, she might have actually made matters worse for Robert when class was over.

She might have tried to make Robert better liked, treating the cause and not just the result. But such efforts must be very subtle, lest the students see through them and add one more reason to their mental lists of how to tease Robert. I suggest that Robert's problem needs to be addressed by his parents rather than his teachers.

If Robert is your child, you are going to spend some distressing days before the two of you escape the junior high years. Robert is going to be unhappy, and I am not sure you can prevent that. You might begin by helping him work on his social skills. Sometimes people need to learn how to take a joke. Or you might try to channel him into a friendship with someone who will accept him.

Or, if the situation is really critical, you may want to give Robert some adultlike experiences or responsibilities that will provide some confidence in himself. These efforts may help, but we can't expect miracles. Once a person gets burdened with Robert's role, it is difficult to break free.

On the other hand, if your child is not like Robert, keep in mind that there probably is a Robert at school. You may want to talk to your junior higher about the problems people like Robert face. The best thing that could happen in this situation would be for one popular person to take Robert's side. If the right junior higher accepted him, it could turn the whole process around. So you may want to talk to your child about his work as a junior high minister witnessing to the divine nature of every creature.

A Personal Example

It's up to you to initiate a discussion with your teenager. No one likes to bring up the topic of his or her own rejection. I know *my* children don't. I discovered this at one of our family discussions which take place on occasional days when we "debrief" during dinner. Doesn't that evoke a nice image? My friendly, happy family sitting around the table, leisurely remembering the events of the day, sharing prayer concerns, stopping occasionally to read a relevant passage from Scripture?

Well, it *is* a nice scene, and at our house we do it regularly. (Notice I said *regularly* instead of *often*. To be honest, we take this opportunity about once a month—whether we need it or not. We have this kind of meal whenever no one has to run off for piano lessons, is late getting home from track practice, or has to get to church for a deacons' meeting.)

"Kris," I asked our seventh grader during one of these events, "when are you going to hear the results of the musical tryouts?"

"She posted them today."

"Oh?" (With junior highers, you sometimes have to use the art of "encouraging listening.")

"Yeah. Dianne got the part."

After some silence, I replied, "Well, Dianne will do a good job."

"Yeah. She can sing better than me."

After some meager attempts to relieve the tension I had created, I suddenly thought of something more positive.

"How's basketball practice?" *That ought to change the tone,* I thought.

"Coach called us in today and said that she would only be able to keep twelve girls."

"Oh?" More encouraging listening.

"I wasn't one of the twelve."

At that moment, I was sorry I *didn't* have a deacons' meeting to rush off to.

Yet, this was a noteworthy night in our family history. Kris had suffered two major setbacks, both in the same day. Despite her lackadaisical attitude and her apparent reluctance to talk about them, she had to be suffering emotionally.

At that point, parents—even those who felt awkward and useless—were valuable to her. Her setbacks provided us not only a challenge but also an opportunity. Here are some things we learned:

1. *We had to help our child manage her hurt.*
To adults who worry about "important" things, not getting into a musical may not seem too shattering. But for a seventh grader, it may represent the loss of all the potential joy in the world. There was no doubt about it. Kris was hurt, and we had to help her manage it.

My first impulse when such things happen to my children (or to yours, for that matter) is to try to heal the hurt—to kiss it and make the pain go away. That's what I would really *like* to do, but I know that I can't.

Kris had suffered some setbacks, and she was going to feel some pain. There wasn't a whole lot I could do to make the hurt go away. And I am not sure that would have been the best thing, even if I could. The natural process of growing inevitably leads to a certain amount of suffering, and that suffering is valuable in helping us become mature.

2. *We had to help her preserve her pioneering spirit.*
Kris had just tackled two challenges. In good faith and with a positive outlook, she had tried to reach into the unknown, to attempt something she had never attempted before. Just trying out for the team and the musical took courage, but both of the challenges had backfired in her face.

Her experimental courage had led only to the pain of rejection.

A normal reaction for someone in Kris's position would be to think to herself, *Oh, well, what's the use? I tried and failed. I won't even bother trying the next time.*

But this is a dangerous attitude, particularly for a seventh grader, and presents one of the greatest challenges to parents. Junior highers have to experiment. That is one of the characteristics of the age. But during experimentation, there are always as many setbacks as successes. Somehow, we have to help our children look objectively at their failures and maintain enough confidence to keep trying.

3. *We didn't burden Kris with unfair expectations.*

The one prayer I pray most frequently as a parent (and a teacher) is that the Lord will give me the wisdom to know how much to expect of my children. If I expect too little of them, they may waste their creative gifts. If I expect too much of them, I may destroy them with an unrealistic burden.

Kris's suffering also caused us pain. We had looked forward to seeing her in the musical, and we had planned to attend the basketball games. But during her crisis, we had to accept our truth and help Kris accept hers.

4. *We had to help Kris get her life back in perspective.*

That night our after-dinner conversation hit on several stories—some from Scripture, some about great heroes, and some about real-life people we knew. We wondered how Zechariah must have handled the suffering of not being able to speak until his child, John the Baptist, was born. We tried to imagine the drive that possessed Glen Cunningham to recover from serious burns and injury to become a world-class runner. We prayed for a young All-American athlete, a friend of the family, who had just learned that because of a latent back injury, he would never be able to compete in gymnastics again.

These memories weren't meant to divert Kris's attention from her own hurts. We retold these stories to remind ourselves that we are never the only people suffering. We used the examples to gain the courage to accept the fact that life is more than speaking and burn scars and gymnastics honors and junior high musicals and basketball. When we have courageous confidence in the truth of the Gospel, life always has hope.

I don't know if Kris learned all that in one night. But at least there weren't any tear stains on her pillow the next morning.

Homework Assignments for Parents

1. If your junior higher is often picked on by his peers, what are some specific ways you can boost his self-esteem at home?

2. If your child doesn't have a problem in this area, how can you motivate him to be a leader in the cause of defending those who are persecuted by unthinking classmates?

3. Does your child talk about the comments and actions that upset him? Does he discuss the people at school who are most persecuted? If you aren't aware of his situation, what are some things you can do to promote honest and open conversation?

Divorce and Its Fallout

itchell and I had become close friends. Since he was quarterback of the seventh-grade football team, we had to spend time together. (You know the bit—the player has to think like the coach.) Those times became precious for both of us. We liked each other. We had some of the same values. We enjoyed each other's sense of duty. Mitchell was a very mature, responsible, well-adjusted seventh grader who was fun to be around—the kind of boy who just had to be a source of joy for his parents.

After football season, even though I only saw Mitchell during class and occasionally in the halls, he was still one of my closest friends. But as winter wore on and both of us got busy, our relationship waned some. I did notice that Mitchell wasn't as jovial in class as he had been, and some of his work wasn't as good as I expected; but I attributed that to snow depression. (As a native Southwesterner, I can understand such things.)

My first cause for alarm came in mid-January. I was called into the office to help the principal with a delicate matter. Mitchell had been caught fighting in the bathroom. Instead of meeting the witty, easygoing, controlled young man I had grown to appreciate, I discovered a calloused, angry person. I could tell that this wasn't a passing mood. Very subtly, there had been a change in his personality, almost a reversal. I decided to interfere, so I called his father. A couple of days later, we met. The father told me about his separation and impending divorce, and he asked for my help during this difficult period. I promised to do what I could.

But as soon as the father reported the conversation to Mitchell, I lost my best friend. That boy sat in class and glared at me. When I turned my back, he made snide remarks under his breath. He approached his assignments with an apathy that looked like resentment.

What had I done to him to earn that kind of treatment? I had entered his secret temple. I had discovered his vulnerability. I knew something about him that he had been trying so hard to hide, and he hated me for it.

No Victimless Divorces

Some writers have projected the idea that children are somehow made to feel responsible for the breakup of their parents' marriage. I don't know whether Mitchell felt responsible or not, but he definitely felt the stigma. He felt unclean.

He tried his best to hide the fact that he was now one of those tragic statistics—a child of a broken home.

I think his hurt went even deeper. Mitchell's father had projected a positive image in the community. He was a leader in business and in his church—a man to be respected and looked up to. In fact, he had played the game of fatherhood according to all the rules. He was a faithful supporter of Mitchell's activities. He made sacrifices to attend ball games. He seemed very interested.

Yet he decided to leave the home and family. At a time when Mitchell was trying to define the meaning of being a man, the one man he had decided to use as a model deserted him. That vacuum, once created, had to be filled with something.

Well-informed people have written some excellent books about the children of divorce, and I won't propose to exhaust the topic in one short chapter; but the subject is relevant to the junior high age. Since the junior higher is already confronted with so many changes, any shift in the stability of the family structure can have a tremendous effect on him. I don't think we can predict how the junior higher will respond, but he will react in some way.

I am not trying to be preachy here, but I am emphatic. In all my years of dealing with other people's children as a teacher, coach, or principal, I have never seen a divorce that had a positive effect on the children, regardless of the problems of the marriage.

If your children are of junior high age, I urge you to think about the consequences of your actions on their development before you make any decisions to alter the family structure, whether that means separating, getting a divorce, or changing family roles.

When Parents Become Peers

Divorce can have other devastating results, as I learned from Heather. I had kept her after school—detention, it's called—for some forgettable breach of etiquette. Since she didn't protest any more than was routine, I concluded that she agreed with my assessment.

Heather reported with her books and started to study. I took advantage of her academic bent and went down to the library. When I got back to the room, she was crying. Since she had been almost agreeable about the detention, I decided it couldn't be the punishment that was upsetting her, so I pried.

Heather told me a disturbing but far too common story. Her mother and father had recently gotten a divorce. Mother immediately reentered dating activities and occasionally brought men to the house for the evening. Since Mother needed someone close to communicate with, she enlisted Heather in the role of companion, consultant, and even confessor.

There were some immediate rewards with Heather's new role. She got some new, grown-up clothes and some good instruction about such things as makeup, men, and flirting. But then Mother became something of a difficult child. She was staying out late at night and sometimes not coming home at all.

All this began to frighten, embarrass, and anger Heather. Sitting in my detention hall, being punished for some serious crime like chewing gum, she began to think about it and cry.

This is a critical situation for any junior higher. Heather simply couldn't handle the role of child and mother at the same time. For a while, being an equal with Mother seemed like a good deal. But in order to get there, she had to give up her right to be mothered, and she just wasn't ready for that. At a time in her life when she was trying to discover her own role, she was faced with too many options. At a time when she was trying to discover what it is to be a grown-up woman, she found herself in competition with her own mother.

Parents: Grow Up!

Although this story is a biting reminder of what can happen in a divorce situation, it has a point for all of us. Most junior highers are simply not mature or stable enough themselves to assume the additional burden of rearing their parents. In other words, junior highers need parents who are able to handle their own adjustments.

If you go to your son's basketball game and don't like the referees, try not to act childish about it. If you have a disagreement with the way a teacher is dealing with your child, make sure your child knows how you plan to deal with the situation before you embarrass him.

Perhaps the greatest psychological need of a junior higher is the need for mature people as models. At the time when these young people are breaking away from childhood and flirting with adulthood, they need someone to show them what being an adult means. If their parents or teachers don't accept the role, they will probably resort to modeling after an older adolescent, and this always carries a risk.

Despite all the flak you may get for wearing something gross like wing-tip shoes or jeans without the right label, and despite the lack of attention you receive when your junior higher is in the company of his compatriots, don't be deceived. He still needs a mature, responsible adult for a role model. He doesn't need a competitor nor a defender. He needs to see how a mature person looks at the world and deals with problems. He needs a parent.

Homework Assignments for Parents

1. If you have been through a divorce, have you tried to get underneath the initial reactions of your junior higher to discover what he is really feeling? Have you established a climate where he feels free to express honest opinions about you and your ex-spouse? Do you ever expect too much from your child in the areas of confiding, consoling, etc.?

2. If divorce hasn't been a problem for you, which of your junior higher's friends could benefit from contact with a strong family unit? When can you take the time to spend with other young people whose parents have been divorced?

SECTION 2: HELPING YOUR CHILD COPE WITH CHANGING FRIENDSHIPS AND PEER PRESSURE

7

Castes and Outcasts

One of the best ways to learn about any wild beast is to study the pack with which it associates. This is particularly true with junior highers, because the grouping is very important to them.

Most junior highers spend a good part of their time and mental energy trying to achieve and maintain some kind of status within a specific social group. Their efforts reveal that it is important to them to belong. Therefore, a study of how any one junior higher behaves and responds will require some analysis of the group that is setting the standards for his thinking, behavior, and appearance.

With some caution about oversimplification and the dangers of generalization, we can classify most junior highers into one of four groups: the Jocks, the Brains, the Regulars, and the Burnouts.

The Jocks

Although in its literal sense the term *Jocks* refers specifically to athletes, in actual operation it has a broader definition. The group usually identified by this term consists not only of the athletes and cheerleaders, but also the students who actively support school activities. (Another title for these people is *socialites*.)

This group is everywhere and into everything. They play sports, lead cheers, print the newspaper, play in the band, get parts in the play, make friends with the teachers, and win all the awards at the annual assembly. They are also active outside school. They are officers in the church youth group; they volunteer for local ministries; they are the leaders in scouts and other community groups.

In other words, they try to find happiness in being productive, active, and cooperative—working within the system rather than fighting against it. Although they encounter the usual frustrations and setbacks, they are basically satisfied with the general quality of life.

They tend to worry about how they look and what adults think about them, so they keep themselves clean according to junior high standards and try to make the best grades they can without earning the label of being scholarly.

In most schools, this is an old, established group. These people have been friends before, so it seems natural for them to stay together during junior high. Although these sweet, innocent children would never intentionally hurt anybody, the group tends to be closed to outsiders. Once this group is established, it's difficult for anyone to break in. (Remember Jessica from Chapter 4? This was the problem she faced.)

The exclusiveness of the Jock Club may present one of the cruelest structures of junior high life. How often I have stayed awake at night and prayed for some poor child who wants to be friends with a cheerleader who is already so popular that she doesn't have time for any more friends! It's not that the cheerleader wants to be cruel—but her tight schedule and limited friendship circle have become the cruelest form of rejection for people who need her attention.

The situation is not quite as rigid for boys as it is for girls. For one thing, boys usually have more opportunities to achieve status than girls do. Any boy who participates in sports can usually make it into this club if he wants, and he might actually rise to a position of leadership just because of his athletic activity.

Although there is a need for experimentation, chance, and risk among the Jocks, the members of this group are usually not as defiant as those of the other groups. They may operate on the fringe of structured rules and procedures, but they aren't really trying to destroy the system or live outside it. After all, the system has provided them with the rewards that help them identify themselves, so they want structure to prevail—even if they have to test it once in a while.

The Brains

I use the label *Brains* to classify a rather select group of junior highers who aren't ashamed to appear intellectual. Although the club isn't sexually exclusive, it tends to be male-dominated.

In many ways the members of this group look and act like normal junior highers (whatever that means). They have growth spurts, voice changes, and skin problems. Like their contemporaries, they fluctuate between childhood and middle age in behavior, attitudes, and interests.

But the Brains differ from the Jocks because they don't have time for all those childish activities such as basketball and cheering. They are simply too busy with chess, poetry, computers, science fiction, intricate science fair projects, or some other intellectual endeavor.

Since this group is smaller than the Jocks, its members tend to build close friendships with each other. If they are unhappy about not being in the popular group, they rarely mention it. On the other hand, members of this crowd may establish some friendships with adults who have similar interests.

Perhaps the most unusual characteristic about the Brains is that they may not make the best grades. Many leave grade success to the Jocks who need the attention, and settle for applying themselves to their private interests.

I once met a junior high girl who had just published a book of poetry. It wasn't quite *Letters from the Portuguese,* but it was still worth reading on a rainy Saturday. Yet when I stopped by her classroom to congratulate her, I had to wait my turn. A teacher was reminding the young author that she was going to earn a D in English for the semester.

The Regulars

In the junior high caste system, the *Regulars* are the equivalent of what politicians once called the silent majority. These are the people who go through life, at least the junior high part of it, without attracting much attention. This is not to say that they don't have their problems. They have as many growth and adjustment struggles as the most active and popular Jock, but since they themselves aren't really big deals to anyone, their problems don't seem like big deals either.

It isn't so much that anyone dislikes them—it's just that no one pays a lot of attention to them. In a typical class situation, the teacher may give as much as eighty percent of his positive reinforcement to the five Jocks, eighty percent of his negative reinforcement to the five Burnouts, and forget the twenty Regulars altogether.

Although they don't distinguish themselves with any great achievements, they don't cause too much trouble, either. They lack the aggressiveness or the confidence necessary to make themselves distinctive in the minds of the people who have the ability to make them important—and most of them don't seem to be too dissatisfied with their lot in life.

The problem is that the standard used to classify a junior higher as a Regular is unrealistic and temporary. Whatever the reasons she is left out of the in group, these reasons may change during this period of transition. And when these changes occur, the Regular needs to have enough confidence in herself to utilize her talents.

If your child gets cut from the seventh-grade basketball team and thus misses his right to be a Jock, you need to encourage him to keep practicing and to keep trying for the next several years. He may grow and mature and be the best high school basketball player in the class. But we won't know that if he lets his early setback destroy him.

Parents must be alert to the danger: Being a Regular can be a self-fulfilling prophecy. If a student learns in junior high that he isn't mature enough to participate in various activities, he may decide never to try again, even after he matures.

Grades can also become self-fulfilling prophecies. Too often students who make C's decide that they are "C people" and go through life expecting C rewards and C opportunities. As parents who love these people for what they are at the moment they come to us, we can't let this kind of categorization internalize within these junior highers. We need to keep encouraging and recognizing the Regulars for what they can contribute.

This warning is particularly appropriate if your junior higher happens to be a middle child or the second child of the same sex. Since we as parents have been through this before, it is difficult to get as excited about it the next time through. Quite unintentionally we may fail to give the second child as much attention, encouragement, or opportunity as the first one got. And the Regular, if he gets dissatisfied with his inconspicuous role, may try to achieve some attention by moving into the world of the *Burnouts*.

The Burnouts

These are the junior high people who have already had so many setbacks and frustrations that they have just decided not to cooperate with the established system anymore. Their protest ranges from overwhelming lethargy to open and hostile rebellion against all structure and authority.

It is difficult to pinpoint the reasons why a young person would make a decision to quit trying to get attention and feelings of self-worth through the system. Perhaps he has a weakness in some learning skill such as reading, or perhaps he is not as good an athlete, or perhaps he is trying to follow the example of some older people, or perhaps he simply prefers this over the more energetic approach to life.

The unfortunate aspect of the junior high Burnout crowd is that many of them are destined to stay there. There are simply not as many options for fourteen-year-olds who have chosen not to participate in the established structure. Once they have made that decision, it is difficult for them to change direction.

For one thing, they get so far behind academically that it is almost impossible for them to catch up. Based on their junior high records, they will be directed into high school classes designed for them and will have fewer opportunities to interact with people outside their group.

If a person doesn't succeed at an activity, after a while he loses interest and quits trying. Eventually he seeks success or at least identification in an alternate activity. If your child meets only constant failure or frustration in class, in school activities, in the church group, or even as your child, he will soon quit trying those activities and search for alternatives.

Somewhere there are people who will accept him for who he is and will provide the companionship and understanding he needs. Somewhere there are people who will convince him that success isn't really that big a deal anyhow and that it's all right not to try. Actually, the group bonding may be stronger for Burnouts than for others. Since no one else accepts them, they accept each other.

The school setting is only a frame of reference. For the most part, junior highers stay in their groups wherever they are. Jocks are Jocks wherever you meet them. Even though a Regular may get a shot a leadership in, say, a church setting if there are no Jocks around, he is still a Regular for most of the time. Most junior highers will internalize their roles in the caste system, and will begin to think of themselves in those roles.

Be Warned

I do present this discussion with all sorts of warnings on the package. Labeling has to be the cruelest of human inventions. I don't think that at creation God said, "I think I will make a Jock this time."

Your child is a unique person who merits your special attention. But at the same time, he does function within the boundaries of a particular social group. If you want to provide your junior higher with some comforting and liberating understanding, you will need to understand something about the characteristics of the group he is in and the group in which he aspires to be.

WHAT PARENTS TRY TO FORGET

Homework Assignments for Parents

1. Which of the four groups mentioned is your child most like? Are you satisfied with his involvement in that group? Or is your inner desire to see him in a different group?

2. How diverse are your child's friends? Does he get along with people from different groups, or does he spend all his time with other members of the same group? Does your junior higher struggle to gain acceptance from others, or is he comfortable in his own "caste"?

8

The Dress Code: Not as Bad as It Appears?

Having defined some of the most common junior high groupings in the last chapter, now we turn our attention to a related topic—junior high costuming. Actually, most junior highers seem to dress according to two standards, peer pressure and individuality.

Although these forces may rub against each other, they are not really as contradictory as they may sound. Peer pressure sets a standard of appearance that is broad enough to allow for individual decoration. For instance, peer pressure may dictate that girls paint their nails, but the choice of color is theirs. Peer pressure may dictate that boys leave the top two buttons open, but the choice of the shirt is theirs.

Or, for an illustration from my generation, peer pressure may dictate that the shirt be pink and the trousers charcoal. The color of the belt, the crowning distinction, was my choice. (And I chose white—the one memory I have retained from my junior high days.)

Since we can't really fix the blame for the way junior highers look, the one thing for parents to understand is that for most of these people, appearance is very important. In fact, it may be as critical at the junior high age as at any period in one's life. Although you may not like the way your child looks, it may be almost necessary for him to look that way. Like the cowboy in the old West, every piece of the costume has a purpose—symbolic if not utilitarian.

Don't Force Issues That Don't Exist

The commitment to appearance seems to provide the junior higher with a sense of security in his constantly changing world, and it permits him a platform to make a statement to a world that isn't particularly interested in what he has to say. Unless the situation gets completely out of hand, I am not convinced it is worth the effort and time to try to fight with a junior higher over the way he looks. Unless your child is indecent or irreverent or unclean, the issue probably doesn't justify the damage to the relationship. I have known families who have drawn the battle lines sharply and fought bitterly, resulting in hard feelings and shaky relationships.

Some things have different meanings for adults than they do for junior highers. Although jeans with holes might mean rags and poverty to us, they may have an altogether different connotation to him; so he doesn't understand our hang-up over his holes.

Actually the dress question points up an interesting matter for parents. We need to stop occasionally and ask ourselves, *Who owns the problem?* If the way your junior higher looks is causing you a problem, you have a right to tell him, "Look, I may be a grouchy old fogey, but we need to understand each other. Let me tell you why I don't like the way you dress, and you tell me why you do. Then we will talk about how we are going to reconcile our differences."

This may not get him out of those worn-out jeans, but that kind of gentle honesty ought to be a bit easier on your ulcer.

Just before our son Larry entered eighth grade, we bought him several pairs of nice pants and some pretty shirts. But in a few weeks, we noticed that he was wearing the same old jeans and shirt every day. We encouraged, pleaded, begged, nagged, and finally ranted, all to no avail.

At Christmas we quietly gave him another new pair of pants and a new shirt. *He can't reject a present*, we thought. Five years later, we found that shirt and those pants tucked far into the back of his closet, still bearing the store tags. But do you know something? Five years later, the issue that provoked all that conflict doesn't seem very important anymore.

Homework Assignments for Parents

1. In what ways does your child's style of dress reflect peer pressure? In what ways does it reflect originality?

2. Do you understand why your junior higher dresses the way he does? Does it bother you? If you are displeased, have you discussed your reasons with him?

3. If you don't endorse the way your child dresses, does it affect your relationship with him? Or are you able to overlook the outside of the person and continue to see the changing, confused, maturing person inside? How can you maintain a constant and understanding relationship with him, while still being honest about your feelings for the way he dresses?

9

Hero Worship, Role Models, and Peer Influence

A mother called me. She was more amused than concerned. Her son, a popular eighth grader, had developed the strange habit of standing around tossing a fifty-cent piece into the air. When he talked on the phone, stood around at home, or waited at the store, he would whip out his well-worn half-dollar and flip it.

Observing this, the mother was rather amused until some of his friends came over to spend the night. They were also flipping half-dollars. How did this new fad get started?

That was an easy question. Early in the year, one of the veteran Phys. Ed. teachers was hospitalized, and we replaced him temporarily with a young professional baseball player who was between seasons. The baseball player was everything an American hero should be—athletic, good-looking, and rich enough for a young man. Besides, he had the romance of stardom. And he had one interesting habit. You guessed it. He stood around flipping a half-dollar. Considering the role he played in the lives of our kids, I am surely glad he didn't chew tobacco.

Junior highers are imitators. Heroes are important to them because they need models, examples, someone to show them the way.

Your junior higher is in transition from childhood to adulthood. Somewhere between the ages of twelve and fifteen he is going to have to surrender much of what he believes, thinks, and needs in order to accept a whole new set of postulates for living his life. To make that transition, he has to study life-styles as they are actually lived. He has to have heroes.

A Startling Survey

One of the best ways to begin to understand your child is to learn something about his heroes, those people he admires. The most efficient way to discover that is to find the proper moment and ask him. In fact, this isn't a bad game to play at home with the whole family. Call in the brood and have them write down the names of the three people they most admire. The answers may startle as well as educate.

Some of my teacher friends survey their junior high students on this subject every year, and the responses fall into a fascinating pattern. Let's see if you can guess what they say.

Rank the following classes of heroes the way you think the junior highers ranked them most frequently in confidential surveys.

____Family members (parents, grandparents, older siblings)

____Peers (other junior high students who are well-known for some reason)

____Teachers

____Publicized figures (entertainers, athletes, politicians)

Would you believe that junior highers select their heroes in just the order they are listed above? An overwhelming majority select a family member as their first choice of a hero or the person that they most admire. Are you surprised? Frightened? Elated?

Given the role that heroes play in the lives of these people, and given the results of these non-scientific surveys, this makes the junior high years a critical time for parents as well as children. Not only do we need to concern ourselves with how our children are making it through the transition, but we also need to examine what we are actually showing them to help them through the trip.

As a parent, you can take the initiative in being a good role model. If you don't, your junior higher may choose another, less trustworthy person to imitate. Let me offer a couple of examples.

The Classroom Power Center

As a visitor in an eighth grade class, I sat at the back and watched the students file in. I picked one guy out immediately, though he didn't seem all that different from everyone else. He was dressed in the standard costume, and he wasn't any bigger than the average student. But Todd came in with an air of assured reserve which indicated that he knew his role in the class and the role he had in the lives of many of his peers. As if by ironic design, he took his seat right in the middle of the room.

The teacher opened the class by reading an e. e. cummings poem she had written on the board. It was a meaningful ditty, packed with imagery and surprise. When the teacher followed with a question, a large guy sitting over near the windows came to life. He held up his hand with that burst of enthusiasm which says, "Call on me, Teach, I've got a better idea than anyone else." Then suddenly, as if he remembered something, he pulled his hand down and turned his head so he could catch Todd in the corner of his eye.

Todd answered the question himself. With a visible sigh of relief, the large guy by the window then lifted his hand, offered a further point, and took an active role in the rest of the discussion. If I were the parent of a boy in that school, the first thing I would want to know is, "Who is this Todd guy who has so much power that the other students have to check with him to see if it is all right for them to enjoy such things as a "mudluscious world"?

When we talk of peer pressure, we usually think in terms of some kind of nebulous mob agreement. But for junior highers, it may be more complex than that. Often, as in this situation, the source of peer pressure may be one person, and the attitudes and activities the rest of the people endorse are directly affected by what that one person thinks and does.

Leadership intrigues me. It is more of an aura than an act—more charisma than content. I have no idea how Todd got his position. Perhaps at one time he could run faster than anyone else. Perhaps he was the first kid on the block to have his own Pac-Man game. Perhaps he could beat them in a fight. Perhaps he had style with the girls. Or perhaps he just had a rare combination of hero qualities. Regardless of where he got his power, he wielded a strong hammer over the lives of those students. For the boys in his class, that one young man was the embodiment of peer pressure.

If your junior higher has a peer hero like Todd, your first task is simply to know who that hero is. Have your child invite him over to the house. Meet him on friendly and frequent terms. You may even call his parents and get together with them on a friendly basis. If this leader is the right kind of person, your junior higher is going to have far less trouble getting through those changing years.

On the other hand, if this leader is the type of person you don't want your child following, you have a different kind of problem. How do you tell anybody that his favorite person is a bum? How do you reason against an adoration that isn't based on objectivity in the first place?

Since you probably can't do much to alter your child's impression of the leader, you have two options. You can take the easy way out and just try to live through the duration. One thing about this kind of a relationship is that it is as fleeting as the junior high years. In a few months, it too will fly away.

But if you feel that you must do something, you may try to work directly with the leader. Again, take the initiative. Invite him into some of your activities. After you get close enough to him, you may earn the right to help him realize the power he has over the lives of others.

In Todd's case, he appeared to be worthy of the respect he had achieved. Anybody who shows interest in e. e. cummings can't be all bad! But now let's take a look at a role model situation that isn't so beneficial to your junior higher.

Older, but Not Wiser

One day a student looked up in the middle of an eighth-grade writing assignment and said, "Mr. Shambles?" (My name is hard to pronounce, but sometimes people make more of a mess out of it than it deserves.) "Mr. Shambles, didja ever see the movie *Porky's* ? Man, it's some flick. Ja ever seit?"

"No, Kevin, I am happy to say that I have never seen *Porky's*. But how did *you* see it? It's R-rated and they shouldn't be letting you in."

"Aw, I went with my friends. They all got cards, and I just snuck in behind 'em. If you go in with people who have cards, they never ask you. They just think you are as old as your friends."

"How old *are* your friends, Kevin?"

"Mostly in high school. A couple are already out."

"You mean they have already graduated?"

"Naw. They quit. You can quit when you're sixteen. These guys have got good jobs. They didn't see any need to go to school anymore."

Since we were in the middle of a writing assignment, this conversation was delivered not only for Kevin and me, but also for the entertainment of the entire class.

Peer acceptance is a tricky business for eighth graders. Some want to be accepted, so they try to look and think exactly like everybody else. Some want to be accepted through the romance of being different from everybody else.

Most want both at the same time. They want to think they are unique and exciting, so they tell stories—real and manufactured—to illustrate their sophisticated uniqueness. But all the while, they really want to meet the criteria for peer approval.

Kevin spoke loudly and enthusiastically enough to make sure he was heard and envied by most of his classmates. He wasn't a bad student. In fact, he was fairly bright. He had good learning skills and he did his work. Despite his rather frequent outbursts of tales documenting the bright-light district of our city, he utilized his time in class efficiently.

It was a good thing, though, because I suspect he wouldn't have had too much time to do homework. He was too occupied with his friends—his older friends—who by now had decided that homework was not one of the priorities of life, and had actually given up the whole school enterprise.

At this point in his life Kevin is headed for trouble. It is bad enough for a junior higher to get into the wrong crowd of peers his own age, but it is especially dangerous when that crowd is several years older than he. (Remember, at this age, three years is a wide space.)

Pros and Cons of Older Friends

The problem with this cross-age friendship is that the younger person is always going to be the follower. In order to stay with the group and maintain the privilege of bragging about it in front of the other eighth graders, Kevin had to do what the others wanted him to do. He had to entertain them. He had to satisfy their need for authority and control in a friendship. He had to respond to their beck and call. He had to slip into the R-rated movies and make the marijuana deals.

His friends were probably thoroughly entertained at Kevin's expense when they bought the beer and got him drunk for the first time. They probably arranged and supervised Kevin's first sexual encounter, and laughed for months afterward when they remembered his awkwardness. Kevin might have been having some degree of fun, but the older "friends" were the real beneficiaries.

Of course, not every cross-age friendship has to be this earthy. I occasionally relate the extreme cases to make my point, but I do think the basic principle is always valid. If your junior high child is running around with an older adolescent, he is not living according to his own moral code. He is living according to the morality of the older friend. If (or when) the opportunity comes for experimenting with alcohol, drugs, sex, dirty books, shoplifting, or joy riding, he won't have the privilege of thinking about whether he *wants* to participate. That decision was made when he identified with the older group.

If you know the older adolescent and have unquestionable trust in him and his judgment, such a friendship may be profitable. Your child could get good moral instruction. If your eighth grade daughter just has to date, you could argue that it would be better for her to go with that nice young sophomore from the church rather than some hooligan her own age. You have a point. But ask yourself first, *Why does that sophomore want to take my daughter out in the first place? Why isn't he interested in a girl his own age? What does he hope to get from this friendship?*

I want to emphasize that young people mature at different rates of speed in different areas—physical, intellectual, emotional, spiritual, and moral. Don't be deceived. A thirteen year old may be mature in some areas of his life, but he is still thirteen years old in others—and a sixteen year old is almost twenty-five percent older than a thirteen year old.

If I have convinced you of the dangers of your junior higher having older friends, I suppose I have the responsibility of telling you how to prevent it. But, as usual, I have more problems than solutions.

Handling a Tricky Situation

Manipulating your child's friendships is not a particularly safe activity. If you don't like your junior higher's selection of friends, your obvious disapproval might be the force that drives them together. So, regardless of how you handle it, you have to be subtle. I suggest prayer, both for yourself and for your child. God promises wisdom if we ask.

In certain cases, a curfew can take care of some of the problem. If your daughter has older friends, they will have to bring her home before the party gets in full swing, and they won't put up with this too long.

Of course, the curfew must be strict enough, and it must be enforced. You'll need the courage to answer the whine, "But nobody else has a curfew. If you loved me and trusted me, you would let me stay out as late as I want to." These lines are not original with your child, but they sure can make you feel tyrannical when seasoned with a little salt water.

But persist. You have logic on your side. People of junior high age simply need more sleep than do older adolescents. Besides, a curfew makes sense from a safety point of view. In this age of rampant and random crime, it is not too much to ask to know where your children are, regardless of their ages. At our house, the curfew is for my peace of mind.

Another way to mellow some of those cross-age friendships is to make sure your child stays busy with junior high functions and junior high people. One of the values of extracurricular activities is that they help the person find an acceptable niche with people her own age. Encourage your junior higher to get into things that permit her to earn the respect and friendship of other junior highers.

Everyone needs to fit in somewhere. If she can't make it in her own age group, she may have to try a group above. You need to do what you can to support your child in activities within her own age group.

If Kevin had been the best basketball player in school, he wouldn't have needed the distinction of having older friends. Since he never played basketball, he had to prove himself another way. Although I never knew his parents, I am sure they would have preferred the inconvenience of supporting his basketball participation over what happened to him as a result of his having to be the clown for his "friends."

My purpose in this chapter has been to present enough different situations to remind you as an interested (and perhaps concerned) parent that your child, during those years between twelve and fifteen, will meet and deal with a variety of social situations that will bend him, amuse him, challenge him, provoke him, and develop him. He will have numerous opportunities to make new friendships that can either have beneficial or devastating effects on his growth. And you can help determine whether this will be a tolerable or a painful experience for him. With enough understanding, mutual love, and prayer, you both can make it through this difficult time of junior high life.

Homework Assignments for Parents

1. Who are your child's role models? How would you classify each of them: A positive influence, a negative influence, or a neutral influence?

2. How are you handling the negative influences in your junior higher's life? Are you doing all you would like to do, or do you feel the need to take a stronger stand against such influences? Specifically, what are the steps you feel you need to take at this point?

3. As you consider your own influence as a role model, what other things should you be doing to help shape your junior higher into the person you want him to become?

10

Lost Possessions: A Different Perspective

The first thing you must learn if you are a teacher or parent of a junior higher is that they never lose anything. I know that for a fact. I coached junior high sports for five years, and never had a player lose a piece of equipment.

But stealing is a different matter. They "steal" from each other all the time. In fact, I heard the following conversation so often I can recite it in my sleep. Just fill in any name. Your own junior higher's may be appropriate.

"Coach, somebody stole my sweat sock."

"What?"

"Somebody swiped my left sweat sock!"

"How do you know it was your left sock?"

"Because it is the one I always wear on my left foot."

"You mean your sock is shaped to fit your foot? How long since you washed your stuff?"

"'Bout two weeks."

"You mean to tell me that somebody stole a sock that had two weeks of your crud on it?"

"They sure did. I put my socks in my locker last night and locked it. Now, when I get here, the left one is gone. Somebody stole it and when I catch him, I'm going to sue." (See how sophisticated junior highers have become recently?)

The thing that startles me about this conversation and the thing it took me years to learn is that this person is serious. In his perception of the situation, someone stole his sock. After all, he is a responsible person. Almost every day he puts his socks in the locker. He has a mental recollection of doing it day after day, and he can't believe that yesterday was an exception.

His only logical conclusion is that some stole the sock. That is the way it has to be. How dare me accuse him of being forgetful or careless! He is in junior high. He is old enough and adult enough to handle responsibility. Forgetting is for children, and I should recognize his maturity.

A Widespread Dilemma

Illustrations of this junior-high attitude are common enough to suggest an epidemic. Recently I visited a school to witness a school-wide locker cleanup. A girl had reported her book stolen, so the principal decreed that every locker would be cleaned and all books would be checked. It turned out later that the girl found her book at home.

A newspaper story tells of a teacher being sued for ordering a strip search of seventh graders. A student reported his small calculator stolen, and the teacher ordered his classmates searched. The student later found his calculator where he had left it—in his book. Of course, the teacher shouldn't have conducted the search, but it does seem sad that he is in all this trouble over a calculator that wasn't really stolen after all.

Perhaps the reason we adults get ourselves in trouble helping these people is that they are so convincing. They believe what they report. There is no way it can be any different from the way it is reported. We have no alternative but to believe them and take appropriate action.

I suppose I ought to conclude this chapter with a practical suggestion or two for dealing with this problem, but I don't have one. I am just reporting it. It exists and it is typical of the age.

I think the mistake in perception grows out of the junior higher's need for others to respect his maturity. I recognize that need, and I am willing to work with it. But it sure can be a nuisance sometimes.

Homework Assignments for Parents

1. What stories can you recall of times that your junior higher's possessions were reported stolen, but turned up later? In retrospect, do you think you handled the situation correctly? Or do you think you should have done something differently?

2. Are you regularly teaching your junior higher to be more responsible? Whenever he blames his failures on someone else or on situations beyond his control (such as losing something), are you too quick to accept excuses? What new ways can you think of to teach him to be more accountable in the future?

SECTION 3: HELPING YOUR CHILD COPE WITH CHANGING ADULT/FAMILY RELATIONSHIPS

11

Testing the Fences

When I glanced in the door, the classroom was in chaos. The young teacher was doing his best to conduct a discussion on some fine point of American History, but the eighth graders were hearing little of it.

Some girls in the back were busy with hair tools and makeup chests, preparing themselves for an afternoon encounter with some high school sophomores who came to our building for basketball practice. Some of the boys, bothered by the girls' insensitivity to their needs for female attention, had swiped one of their purses and were playing a rather competent game of keep-away. Three or four other boys were playing with a beeping computer game. The more attentive students occasionally interrupted their own personal discussions to answer one of the teacher's questions with a smart reply, designed to bring tons of hilarity to all within earshot.

As principal, I could have gone in, stopped the mess, and restored order. The students would have respected my office enough to respond to my presence. For one thing, they knew I had the ability to "get them into trouble." But I decided against going in. My presence would only have served to undermine what little authority the young teacher still had. There had to be a better way to help him and the class through this adjustment period.

I wandered on down to my office, expecting a "visitor" from the history class. Sure enough, in about ten minutes, Scott walked through my door. That in itself interested me. The whole class had been in an uproar. How could that young teacher have singled out one individual who was solely responsible for the general chaos? Of course, I knew what the teacher was doing. He had to take some measure of action, so he picked out the most vocal person to serve as an example.

"Scott," I asked, "are you in trouble again?"

"Yeah, but it's not my fault."

"What's not your fault?"

"It's not my fault that I'm in trouble."

"Why isn't it your fault? You *are* in my office."

"It's not my fault, because he's a lousy teacher."

"What do you mean, he is a lousy teacher?"

"He can't control the classroom."

"But, Scott, I just came from your classroom, and you were the worst one in there."

"That's what I said. He can't control me. He's a lousy teacher, and I shouldn't get in trouble just because he can't control the class."

Now figure that one out. What was Scott trying to tell me with that piece of logic? What lesson can we learn?

Actually, it seems obvious enough. Scott and the rest of the class were simply trying to find the fences. They were looking for boundaries.

They didn't really like that chaotic situation any more than the teacher did, but they were depending on him to establish the guidelines. When he, through his inexperience, failed to do so, the class had to keep flailing until someone imposed some limits. For these eighth graders, this was a form of experimentation.

Freedom within Boundaries

Scott did not have the personal discipline to build his own fences. He needed some kind of external authority curtailing his behavior. When he couldn't find it, he became frustrated and angry. Although he kept experimenting, he would have felt better about the situation if he had bumped into the boundaries *before* his behavior actually got out of hand. He wasn't pleased with himself, but he knew he wasn't to be blamed. It was the teacher's fault.

Although Scott probably would have complained about the boundaries when they were first explained to him, he would have abided by them once he knew they were fixed. And he would have been happier for it because, in a strange, paradoxical way, he would have had more freedom.

Try that one on for size. *The more rigid the boundaries, the more freedom he would have had within the boundaries.* That is not an absolute or universal principle, but it is applicable to a majority of situations. Most junior highers are simply trying to discover how strong the fences are.

This is a point that may confuse young teachers and parents. In order to find out where those fences are, the junior higher has to experiment; he has to test; he has to war against the boundaries themselves to make sure they are real and not just inconvenient facades.

In other words, the junior higher's normal reaction is to complain about the rules and restrictions. If you listen to him, you may get the idea that he really resents their being there. But usually, all that complaining and testing is just the junior higher's way of finding out where the real boundaries are. Once he settles that point, he will probably be content to live within the boundaries or accept the consequences for violating them.

It is appropriate for your thirteen-year-old child to say, even in loud and animated tones, "I don't want to go to Grandma's house for Thanksgiving. I am *not* going to Grandma's house for Thanksgiving. You can't *make* me go to Grandma's house for Thanksgiving. There is absolutely *nothing* for me to do there. I'm going to stay home and go over to Jill's and listen to records and run around all day. But I am *not* going to Grandma's house!"

Let me repeat: it is perfectly appropriate for her to say that. It isn't meant to be a personal attack on you or Grandma. It is simply your child's way of saying, "Are you serious? Do you *really* want me to go to Grandma's house for Thanksgiving?"

How you respond to this bit of testing fences depends on your personality. I, since it is appropriate with my style, would resort to firm levity: "Ha-ha. You're such a funny person. To think that I could spend Thanksgiving at Grandma's without you. You're so funny, we have to have you in the car for entertainment, or none of us could make the trip. Yep, as I think about it, I do believe you *will* go to Grandma's house for Thanksgiving."

Now, I know the risk I am running here. She will go, but she may not be much fun to be around. Nevertheless, we have at least established the boundaries. Since I have settled one question for her, I have now provided her with the freedom to experiment in other areas. Despite all her complaining, she prefers this to chaos.

So let me conclude with a summary and a warning. First the summary:

1. *Don't be afraid to set the boundaries.*
You are the adult in the relationship. Your child is looking for some guidance. Give it to her.

2. *Don't be shocked by all the testing of the boundaries once they are in place.*
How else will she know that you are really serious?

3. *Keep your word despite the testing.*
Be firm. If she violates the boundaries, make sure she accepts the preestablished consequences.

And now for the warning. Not all junior highers are just testing to see where the fences are. Some are actually squeezed in by the structure and are lodging a deeper form of protest. Many of the points in this chapter and in this book are generalities. They fit most junior highers, but I urge you to stay close enough to your own child to discover in what ways he or she is unique and doesn't fit the mold.

The exciting challenge of being a parent of a junior higher is the demand for creativity. By watching the group we can make some general observations and plan some specific strategies. But since every day brings changes, we constantly have to rearrange and redirect. Just as the junior higher learns by experimentation—trial and error—so parents can learn too. And we get to learn all over again with each child, because no two are alike.

Isn't parenting exciting as well as educational!

Homework Assignments for Parents

1. Have you set established boundaries for your junior higher? Does he know what to expect if he intentionally ventures outside of those boundaries? Are you clear in communicating when you feel this has taken place?

2. On the other hand, do you encourage the exercise of freedom within those boundaries? Do you help him find new ways for self-expression and growth before he begins to "test the fences" on his own?

12

Family Relationships: A Necessary Nuisance

"**B**ut, Daddy, we've just *got* to go tonight!"

"Oh?"

It's going to be a great concert. Our band and orchestra are really good."

"Oh." I am a little cautious about accepting a junior higher's opinion on musical quality. I hear those sounds seeping out of her room.

"All my friends are going to be there."

"Oh." Now we are getting to the real reason, and I suspect she is about to pull out all the big guns.

"Besides, it would be a great family activity. Wouldn't it be fun for the *whole family* to go somewhere together? What would be better than the school spring musical concert?"

Now, that one makes sense. Families do need to spend time together, and I am encouraged to see her think of her younger brothers and sisters for a change. Most of the time she treats them with an aggressive indifference.

So after dinner we load her and the little ones into the car and travel over to the junior high school for the concert. But as soon as we pull into the parking lot, she bolts out the door and runs into the building. She spends the evening sitting halfway across the auditorium from us and is waiting at the car when the whole affair is over. This is what she calls a family outing.

War and Peace: The Parent Version

I don't know whether she is ashamed of us or not. Perhaps we do cramp her style. I guess we are not as romantic or ideal as the movie models. Maybe we do embarrass her. But whether she is ashamed or not, we are definitely a nuisance now that she is learning how to fly on her own, be her own person, take responsibility for her emotions and actions, and manage her own social relationships.

At this point, she really doesn't need interference from us. Besides, to be seen in public with her parents might seriously damage her reputation of independence. In addition to that, having her parents around demands some social graces that don't yet come easily. Just handling introductions can be an embarrassing situation. Trying to remember which person to mention first and then trying to think of the name to use for her parents is worth a giggle or two. When she introduces us to her friends, does she call us Momma and Daddy or the more embarrassing formal titles of Mr. and Mrs. Schimmels?

Of course, that little show of independence may not be limited to public display. She may even try it out at home occasionally. On the list of things that baffle parents, this is probably number one. Most of the people I talk with simply can't understand that age-old dependent-independent paradox.

At one moment, our children are begging us for independence and are vociferously objecting to any parental interference in their lives. The next moment they come with their childlike needs to be filled from the parents' fountain. Just trying to decide when to hold on and when to let go is enough to drive any normal parent into a state of terminal stress.

So maybe the solution is not to worry about it. Just keep the relationship constant. Despite all her running around to avoid us at the concert, despite all her pleas for her own TV set so she won't have to be in the same room with us, despite all her plans for an "unchaperoned" party at our house, we just keep going on about this business of being parents as we always have.

We won't panic. We won't yell. We won't even demand our rights or threaten her with independence, since that is what she seems to want. We will just keep loving her and letting her know that we love her.

In a couple of years—or maybe ten or twenty—she will need us again, and we will still be there. And we'll be ready to remind her of this concert experience when she goes through the same thing with our grandchildren.

War and Peace: The Sibling Version

But while we as parents can usually be patient, understanding, and forgiving while our junior higher is growing up, we can't always say the same for all the siblings involved. To older brothers and sisters, a junior higher is a nuisance—a mere child going through the silliness, awkwardness, and rebellion of transition, who lacks the sophistication or opportunity for excitement that an older age offers. She is always struggling to be something she isn't in order to fit in where she doesn't. At best, she is to be tolerated.

On the other hand, to younger brothers and sisters, the junior higher can easily become a hero. To them, her life does have variety and excitement. When someone is ten years old, what could appear more adult and brazen than shifting classes every hour, not sitting with your parents during church, going away on a retreat, buying your very own record album, or wearing eye makeup? But regardless of the junior higher's family role (somewhere between hero and heel), she is probably confused by it.

Junior high is a time for social adjustments, for learning how to manage affairs with a variety of people in a variety of situations. The relationship with brothers and sisters is just another test.

Despite how special family relationships may be, her responses to the demands of those relationships will still probably come from within her scope of dealing with any other social relationship. In other words, you can probably expect her to try to manage affairs with her brothers and sisters with some of the same techniques that she uses with anyone else. Let's review some of those.

Experimentation—Since she is trying to discover what emotions and feelings are appropriate for everyone she meets, she needs to try out several. One day, the junior higher may be cooperative and supportive of her little brother. The next day, she may ignore him. One day she may admire an older sister. The next day she may attack her with painful verbal darts.

Cruelty—Not all junior highers are cruel, and no junior higher is cruel *all* the time. Yet cruelty is a rather common characteristic of some relationships. Junior highers use cruelty as an expression of frustration and as an attempt to achieve a degree of self-distinction. Don't be surprised if your junior higher tries a little cruelty while dealing with her siblings, regardless of whether they are older or younger. But just because you understand why she tries that method doesn't mean you have to approve of it. If you don't like her cruelty, put a stop to it. Just be sure to avoid using cruelty to attack cruelty.

Isolation—Often, the junior higher finds relationships outside the home more fulfilling than those inside the home. You may not understand that. You might think you are doing everything possible to make sure she knows she is loved and cherished. In fact, you may get the idea you are a bad parent and that you should increase family activities and rituals in an attempt to deal with her rejection of you. But it may not be necessary. If the bonds and activities that hold your family together are not as strong as they need to be, I encourage you to strengthen them, regardless of your children's ages.

Participation and Privacy

As parents you have a right to maintain family functions during your junior higher's period of personal adjustment. You have a right to demand that she eat meals with the family, take family trips, and do her chores. You can insist that she maintain her family position, yet still give her privacy. There is no need to panic just because your junior higher spends all her time in her room behind a locked door. She needs some privacy, and you should respect that.

Another key for parents is to make sure we keep spreading the family glue, even when the splits may seem wide and permanent. Usually the glue that holds families together is like cement. Once it is set and allowed to dry, it gets better with age.

When my children were in junior high, I thought that I would be a successful parent if I could just manage to keep them from killing each other. I suspected they would never speak to each other again once they had flown from the nest. But now that they are young adults, they are close friends, cherishing each other's company.

If you bear with your junior highers when they are going through their experimental, cruel, isolated stage, you may be surprised at how well they turn out.

Homework Assignments for Parents

1. In what ways does your child suggest that you as a parent are occasionally a nuisance? In what ways does he continue to show that he needs you? How well do you handle the mix of expressions?

2. What things do you need to do to ensure that your junior higher maintains a balance between independent activities and family functions?

3. How well do you oversee the relationships between your junior higher and any brothers or sisters? Do you wait until you receive complaints, or do you address instances of cruelty as they happen?

13

The Fourteen-Year-Old Defense Attorney

"**S**ally, I don't care if you were absent yesterday. You will have to take the test today. You've known about it for two weeks."

"You can't do that," yells out Karen from across the room.

"I beg your pardon." Here I am trying to have a quiet conversation with Sally, and I find myself debating her self-appointed defense attorney.

"It isn't fair. She wasn't here yesterday," Karen continues.

"But she knew about it for two weeks." *Why am I defending myself to this spectator?*

"It still isn't fair. She should be allowed to go to the library today and take the test tomorrow."

By now the young barrister has convinced the jury, and twenty-five heads are nodding assent while I stand there wondering how I got tricked into open debate in the first place.

Perhaps this event would make sense if Karen were Sally's best friend, but she isn't. I'm not sure the two even speak to each other. Or maybe it would make sense if Karen didn't like me, but I think she does. We have pleasant conversations, and she does good work with a minimum of complaints. So what is the issue?

It Isn't Fair!

The issue is actually quite simple for junior highers. Karen has reached an age during which she can't tolerate injustice. As a rather intellectually mature eighth grader, she wants things to make sense. She wants people to treat each other according to the rules of human decency. She wants logic and justice to prevail.

Since she didn't think I was being logical in Sally's case, she, with her duty to justice, was called upon to champion the underdog. On a different occasion she might support me against the students, even if her stand made her unpopular. But this time she thought I was wrong.

Although I can understand how Karen might be a nuisance at home at times, she is fun to have around. It is refreshing to see a person at any age embrace this duty to justice, but it is rather typical of junior highers.

Of course, their approach to justice sometimes comes equipped with some interesting characteristics that make it even more charming. For one thing, junior highers like their justice to be simple and pure. They aren't too interested in the complexities of compromise. Right is right, and it is the only thing that matters.

But at the same time, the junior higher's sense of justice is often a bit egocentric. He first wants to make sure he is treated fairly, and then he may have time to worry about his peers. After that, he may be able to handle some concerns for a bigger world.

Why? When? Why Not? Where?

I include this description of junior high justice for two reasons. First, I want to remind you that for the first time since your child was born, you may have to include a reason for every piece of instruction. Junior high is the age when the person wants to know the why of every action and decision.

Second, I want to prepare you for some of the questions you may have to answer. Here's a sampling.

1. You said we would go tonight. Why have you broken your word?

2. Why do I have to have a curfew just because my older sister stayed out too late when she was my age?

3. You said I could paint my nails any color I wanted, and I happen to like chartreuse.

4. Why doesn't the president just cancel welfare and make all those people go to work?

5. If you can buy a Fuzzbuster for the car, does that mean I can cheat on tests as long as I don't get caught?

6. I don't see why it was wrong. Nobody caught me.

7. But Daddy, I *tried* to call my art teacher Mr. Smith, but he told us to call him Charlie.

8. I don't see why I have to learn grammar. People can understand me when I talk.

9. Why do I need to make good grades? I can always go to college *somewhere* just as long as I graduate.

10. How old were you when you started dating?

11. I don't see how smoking marijuana is any worse than getting drunk.

12. Show me *where* the Bible says it's wrong.

13. If I lived in some of those poor countries, *I* wouldn't starve. I would get a job.

14. I don't see *why* I have to sweep the floor. It just gets dirty again.

15. It's not fair. I had to do the dishes *last* night.

These are just a few of the many questions you may be called on to answer during these wonderful years when your child is in the process of putting away childish outlooks and innocence. Do you have the answers to all of them? If so, I hope you're available for me to call on the next time I need adequate replies that will satisfy the junior highers *I* know.

Homework Assignments for Parents

1. In what ways is your child's sense of fairness developing? Are you pleased to see signals that he cares about justice, or does his attitude cause problems for you?

2. How can you use your junior higher's sense of fairness to your own benefit? For example, if he insists that everyone treat him fairly, surely you have the right to point out (in a firm but gentle way) the times when he treats you unfairly. Make a mental note of any recurring settings where you might have the opportunity to say something at a time when he will get the point clearly.

SECTION 4: HELPING YOUR CHILD CONTINUE TO LEARN

14

Lessons on Learning

The teacher read the poem:

Flower in the crannied wall,
I pluck you out of the crannies,
I hold you here, root and all, in my hand,
Little flower—but *if* I could understand
What you are, root and all, and all in all,
I should know what God and man is.
(Alfred, Lord Tennyson)

Anticipating a great discussion, she looked up from the book and phrased the first question, "Now, class, what do you think the poet means when he speaks of the wall?"

One young man answered for the whole eighth grade. "He means a wall."

"No," she protested ever so gently, "let's go deeper. Let's get beneath the words he used. What do you think he wanted the wall to stand for?"

"How do you know it stands for anything? Maybe the author was just talking about a wall."

His classmates nodded their approval.

"No." The teacher tried to hide her exasperation. "I think he was trying to say something else. To say something deeper."

"Well, why didn't he say it then? Everybody is always talking about how poets are trying to say this or that, and it seems to me that if a person wanted to say something, he would just say it outright. How can we expect to know what he was trying to say unless he tells us?"

At this, the teacher closed the book and dreamed of life in the South Seas. Unfortunately, her college professors had neglected to tell her about eighth-grade reasoning when she was preparing to be a teacher.

Concrete vs. Abstract Thinking

That student and his supporters weren't trying to be anti-intellectual; they were just seeing the world from their point of view. Just about the time they are beginning to understand the surface world, someone was trying to tell them that there is a whole other world beneath that structure. They decided to protest that possibility until they could get a better handle on things.

I offer no prescription here—just the information. But all of us who deal with junior highers need to remember it. Psychologists tell us that we should be able to expect people to move from concrete thinking to more abstract thinking during their junior-high years—to move from number lines to mathematical formulas, from walls to symbols. This shift in perspective does not come without difficulty.

As we live our lives as models to them and as we talk of things like truth, justice, and fairness, we need to realize that junior highers tend to see and understand such things at the most basic level. If they miss our point the first time, we may need to help them think through the concept or rephrase our statements in a way they would understand.

Special Interests

But sometimes if we aren't communicating on the same level as our junior highers, it could be that they are smarter than we are. Let me explain.

One time I was observing an English class taught by a rookie teacher just out of college—a mere wisp of a girl. The lesson for the day was a class participation drill in the uses of nouns in sentences. Despite what you might think, the students were actually excited about it, and they were doing their best to get things right for the young teacher.

Finally, it was Brad's turn. "Give me," the teacher said, "a sentence using a noun as a direct object." Almost as if he were seizing an opportunity, Brad answered, "In 1951, Bobby Thompson hit the shot heard 'round the world."

As it turned out, Brad and I were the only two people in that room who knew he had used a perfectly acceptable example of the grammatical principle in a good sentence, full of poetic allusion. Of course, neither the teacher nor any of the students knew what he was talking about.

I was the only person there old enough to remember or care about such things as the New York Giants and Brooklyn Dodgers, so Brad's recitation of "ancient history" went almost unappreciated. But at least he had found an opportunity to let his hobby creep into his schoolwork.

Now, this is the same fellow who earlier in the day couldn't remember the capital of North Dakota for a geography test and couldn't spell *botany* on a science exam. But he knew his baseball. He knew the date and facts concerning Bobby Thompson's historic accomplishment. He could tell you the names, clubs, batting averages, and salaries of everyone currently playing. He could go back into the golden years and remember when the enterprise of baseball was still a sport.

Actually, the Brads are rather common in junior high. They are not to be confused with the intellectuals. For the most part, they don't care all that much about things like history and science and direct objects. They have simply established themselves as experts on one subject—cars, rock-and-roll music, sports, animals, the Civil War.

Handling Hobbies

Although this kind of intense hobbying can be something of a trial, particularly when you are trying to get the garbage carried out, it is still a rather healthy activity. I would much prefer to see a student interested in baseball instead of one not interested in anything. In fact, I think it is wholesome for parents and teachers to encourage this kind of thing even though the hobby may detract from studying and chores.

Now that I have given you that piece of persuasion, I must admit that I don't really know how to promote hobbies, especially intense ones. People get into them and cherish them for various reasons.

Some junior highers seem to follow the lead of their parents or some other close adult, while others tend to rebel against family activities and search for something that is distinctively theirs. Some junior highers respond to direct suggestions, while some prefer to think they have come up with the idea themselves. Some junior highers like to have a hobby with high visibility, while others prefer to keep a low profile.

So from this variety of preferences, we reach one conclusion: Be careful of generalities.

On the other hand, it is important for parents to realize the value of a hobby and to help the junior higher protect it. You're probably more noble and less compulsive than I am, but if Brad were my son, I would have to fight against the urge to punish him through his hobby. "If you miss curfew one more time (or if your grade doesn't come up), I am going to take those baseball cards from you and put them away for three years."

Of course, that's a foolish statement for a couple of reasons. For one thing, the threat isn't reasonable. Any normal child will say to himself, *Three years? Don't be absurd.* But also, it will be advantageous to both of us for him to keep his interest in that hobby. He will be happier, more active, and more creative going through the junior high years, and we will always have a point of reference.

You *can* communicate with junior highers if you know the rules. First, be warned that they have trouble comprehending abstracts. And second, try to identify with at least one of their hobbies that can help you determine their thoughts and feelings.

It just so happened that I listened to a lot of ball games on the radio in 1951, and I am going to get a great deal of pleasure telling Brad about the one that he has only read about.

Homework Assignments for Parents

1. Has your child had trouble relating to certain abstract issues? If so, how can you describe the same issues in more concrete terms?

2. What hobbies interest your junior higher? Can you identify with one or more of them in order to strengthen your relationship by sharing interests? Do you have common interests from which you can begin a new hobby together?

15

Learning about Sex

Here comes Emily down the hall, holding hands as usual. This time it's with Rick. A couple of days ago, she was walking arm in arm with Greg. I don't think she's being too selective at this point; she just likes boys, and she seems to like having them touch her.

Obviously, her social antics are a real nuisance in the classroom. There is probably nobody as eager for female attention as an eighth grade boy, and nobody as awkward with it. But beyond that, I worry about Emily. Watching her public display of affection, I shudder to think what is happening privately.

I will accept the argument that physically Emily is more woman than child, and I realize that in some cultures she would probably be married and on her way to motherhood by now. But that is not the way it works here.

Nature says they are adults, but culture says they are children. The junior highers might sense that something is unfair about all this, but those are also the facts of life. When junior highers suddenly realize their sexual potential, society tells them not to use it.

I could play amateur psychologist and guess all the reasons for Emily's cravings. Maybe she is lacking something or looking for something or protesting something. Regardless of the reasons, Emily's actions are about to lead to some rather serious consequences. She is headed for trouble. Although we may not be able to prevent Emily's needs, we can at least teach her how to deal with them.

Somebody Had Better Say Something

With increased sexual power comes increased curiosity. Emily is in urgent need of sex education. I don't know where she is going to get her training, but she needs it. If she doesn't get a formal study, she is going to get an informal one quicker than we want her to. Somebody had better provide her with counseling, direction, and understanding.

I realize that this is an unpopular subject. Schools may attempt a bit of sex education, but their efforts are almost always limited to issues of fact. The subject is deeper than that. And if the school's attempts are inadequate, studies indicate that parents aren't doing much better.

Recent surveys maintain that fewer than twenty percent of high school students have received any sex instruction from their parents. That leaves about eighty percent of the nation's children to learn on the streets or from the activities that follow such things as holding hands in the halls.

If Emily were my daughter, I would swallow my pride, muster my courage, and begin a long series of serious discussions with her (in spite of how much I hate such encounters). Of course, I just wouldn't blurt it out. I would try to create a tender time—some occasion when she is pleased to be my daughter and I am pleased to be her parent, when both of us are feeling good and acting like adults. But I would get into the conversation soon.

Whether she gets the information and understanding from her parents or some other source, Emily needs to learn several lessons.

1. *She needs to understand how her body works.*

Although I put this first on the list, I do so with some reservation. Unfortunately, most sex education not only starts but ends here. It simply isn't enough. The whole business of human sexuality is a complex issue, and when your junior highers first discover it, they are going to need some help to understand how it works, how the impulses affect the body, and how conception occurs.

These facts are part of the mystery and beauty of God's creation. If junior highers do not learn about their own bodies within that framework, they will still make the discoveries— but those discoveries will have a different meaning.

WHAT PARENTS TRY TO FORGET

2. *She needs to understand the moral code.*

I always get accused of being a sexist when I say this, but I'll say it anyway: most junior high males are going to depend on the females to establish the sexual rules. If the girl is willing, the guy almost always is. Emily's hand-holding partners will go as far as she permits them. This may seem like an unfair burden of responsibility to put on the females, but it is there. Emily—and your daughter—need to know about it.

3. *She needs to try to understand her own emotions.*

I am a parent, too, and I would really like to ignore the fact that my teenager is feeling all those emotions connected to an awakening and growing sexuality. I would like to think that she is immune to them, that I have taught her so well that those emotions are somehow counteracted by more important things to think about. I would like to believe all that, but I know it isn't true. So I must help her understand where those emotions come from and how to live with them.

4. *She needs to understand the consequences of sexual activity outside of marriage.*

Anybody who engages in sex at this age is going to inherit a plethora of problems. Emily needs to hear about those.

5. *She needs an honest relationship with a responsible adult.*

One of the by-products of a good discussion with your junior higher could be that the two of you grow closer as you talk. Such honesty is needed. Emily isn't mature enough to accept her emotions or their consequences. She needs help in understanding herself, but in order to get it, she needs to feel comfortable discussing herself. Take the initiative and start the relationship.

6. *She needs to realize the biblical mandate to fidelity.*
   The Bible is filled with texts that teach us this great principle. What you select is a matter of choice. Personally, when that time comes for me to gulp for fresh air, turn purple, stammer, and perform my fatherly duty of talking to my children about the beauty of sexuality, I start with Ephesians 5. I want to couch the whole discussion in the image of a model of love—the love of Christ for His bride, the church.

We need for our junior high sons and daughters to catch a glimpse of this kind of total love before they plunge into a relationship that makes a mockery of it. And we need to ensure that we are never guilty of withholding essential information from them simply because we are uncomfortable discussing it.

Homework Assignments for Parents

1. Have you and your junior higher had regular, open discussions concerning sex? Do you make it easier for him to talk about it by initiating the discussion and being the first one to be honest?

2. How much do you know about the sexual activity of your child's classmates? Does he tell you what goes on at school with other couples— good and bad? How might you guide one of your discussions of sex in general into a conversation on the personal aspects?

3. Is your discussion of sex balanced between the factual/biological aspects and the moral/spiritual considerations? Both should be important to your child at this stage. Are you encouraging questions in both areas?

16

Learning about Drugs and Drinking

L isa is a junior higher who would never think of using drugs. All her life she has been bombarded with accurate information documenting the perils of drugs and the consequences of drug use. Since she is a sensible girl, she has made a firm commitment to keep her body free of anything that can cause that much damage. She may be at the experimentation age when she will try about anything, but she won't try drugs. The risk is just too great.

Besides, taking drugs is not a very acceptable activity in Lisa's crowd. Lisa is a popular student, involved in school activities. She cooperates with the teachers and makes good grades. None of the people she knows well are into drugs. They leave that sort of thing to the Burnout group.

During the spring of her seventh grade, Lisa spent the night at a slumber party with three or four of her friends. As the evening wore on and the girls began to get silly, they decided to make things exciting by experimenting with some tricks they had heard about. They first tried to pass out by breathing deeply ten times and then having someone push the rest of the air out. After this game didn't produce any great earthshaking results, the hostess proposed another measure.

Since the family was asleep, she would sneak into her father's liquor supply and get something for them to drink. Through stifled giggles, they executed the crime, and each girl drank enough to begin to feel a bit woozy. This ordeal provided them with embarrassment, chuckles, and grown-up secrets for the next couple of weeks.

But when the group planned the next slumber party, they all naturally assumed that liquor would be a part of it. It had been so much fun the time before, and it seemed so innocent. What harm could come from it? Besides, a couple of girls had watched their parents drink in the meantime, and they were eager to demonstrate what they had learned about the art.

This is how it all started—at a slumber party. Yet this little band of girls had now been introduced to alcohol. Soon drinking became a part of their social activity. By the time they were half-way through eighth grade, Lisa and her friends were finding some opportunity to get tipsy as often as once every two weeks.

Lisa has a drug problem.

The #1 Drug

When I talk with parents, I sense a rather universal fear of drugs. Parents, and I am included in this group, tremble at the mention of such words as *marijuana, crack,* or *cocaine.* We all want to know how we can keep our children away from these dangerous elements. If you have reason to suspect that your child is already involved in any of these, you need far more information than I can provide in one short chapter. See a counselor. Get help.

Yet while you are spending so much of your time and energy trying to protect your children from "drugs," don't forget how easy it is for them to get introduced to alcohol—the most widely abused drug in the country, and the most common drug among junior highers.

Junior high educators who care about their students' personal lives consider alcohol use to be the most urgent concern for school people and parents alike. For one thing, drinking is so widespread because alcohol is easy to get.

If Lisa were getting tipsy on cocaine as often as she were on alcohol, someone would find out fairly soon. That kind of habit would play havoc with the weekly allowance. But she *can* find alcohol on a regular basis.

In addition to being available and affordable, alcohol seems to some junior highers to be safe. Lisa is a sensible girl. She would not intentionally harm herself. She and her friends were not reacting against anybody or anything. They were just experimenting with a new activity. It didn't appear to be dangerous; after all, they know a lot of nice people who drink occasionally.

Message in a Bottle

At this point, you may ask, "Yes, but is alcohol really as dangerous as the other kinds of drugs that we worry about? Are we making too big a deal out of a bit of innocent drinking?"

I don't want to get into any argument that would require comparing the dangers of one high against another, but the facts about teenage drinking frighten me. They convince me that I don't want my fourteen year old at the stage where Lisa was during her year in eighth grade. Let me list some of those facts.

1. *Alcohol is addictive.*

I shouldn't need to say much here. This is documented truth.

2. *Alcohol dulls the brain and impairs judgment.*

With as many challenges as life itself presents to junior highers, they don't need the added burden of going into any experience half-armed.

3. *Alcohol relaxes social inhibitions.*

During this age of experimentation, when the junior higher is trying to develop his own moral code and test the fences, he really doesn't need any foreign substance to give him a false sense of courage. When my child gets to the point of making some decisions about what he will or will not do, I want him to remember clearly everything I have ever taught him about how to behave.

4. *Alcohol use often has unpleasant consequences.*

There are too many stories of tragic automobile accidents for me to ignore the dangers of teenage drinking. When those people involved are only facts in the newspaper, we tend to be rather philosophical about the whole thing. But when someone we know is injured or killed, we suddenly realize that teenage drinking does destroy the lives of some very precious people.

In my years as a teacher, I have lost some of my closest friends through teenage drinking bouts. That is why I am so worried about Lisa.

An Alternative to Alcohol

If I have convinced you that alcohol use is a potential danger for your junior higher, I have achieved my major goal in this chapter. I want you to think seriously about that possibility, and I want you to consider what you can do to help your child through this period of temptation. For that mission, I do have a few suggestions. These may not be applicable in all situations, and the list may not be comprehensive enough to cover all possibilities, but at least you will have some vehicle of action through which you can direct your concerns.

1. *Know when your child first uses alcohol and every time he uses alcohol.*

I like giving advice. It is so easy. I can matter-of-factly tell you *what* to do, but deciding *how* to do it will be much more of a problem for you. Still, I am serious. If you are really concerned about your child's relationship to dangerous drugs and you truly want to be instrumental in his decisions about them, you must have a strong enough relationship that the two of you can be honest with each other.

This is the key. There aren't any shortcuts. There is no easier way. If you don't have such a relationship, find the time to establish one.

2. *Present the facts about alcohol.*

As I said at the beginning of the chapter, the distribution of information concerning the dangers of drugs seems to be having some effect. After so long, people do respond to the facts. Give your child the truth about alcohol, and make sure you don't try to manipulate the facts for any reason.

3. *Show your child how to live a happy, pleasant, fun-filled life without alcohol.*

There are enough sources around promoting the drinking option—TV, his friends, even his sports heroes. To counteract this influence, he needs some trusted models to demonstrate that he can manage his life without artificial highs. Remember: he is at the age when he demands that advice be based on example. Let me put this thought into a question: Would you be pleased if your junior higher had the same attitude toward drinking that you have?

In fact, as I conclude this chapter on drugs and alcohol during the junior higher's development, this question, paraphrased and generalized, becomes a theme. As my own children grow older, I am beginning to realize the validity of some of the biblical promises regarding child rearing. If we teach what is right (with words *and* deeds), if we pray faithfully, and if we are patient, God has promised to regard those efforts. So I ask once again: Will you be pleased if your child lives his life according to what you have taught him?

Homework Assignments for Parents

1. How much do you know about drug use in your junior higher's school? Do you need to discuss the issue with teachers or counselors?

2. What is your child's attitude toward drugs? What is his attitude toward drinking? Are you providing him with factual information in addition to your own opinions and instructions?

3. What personal stories concerning drinking (about yourself or friends) can you share with your child to supplement the facts and statistics he is hearing?

17

Learning to Schedule Activities

"Now, Mom, let's make sure you've got it straight. I'll stay after school for cheerleader practice, but you will need to pick us up at four-thirty and take us to the library so we can work on the science fair project. Then at seven, when you come to the library, bring a sandwich with you, and I'll eat it on the way to church for the youth sing."

The junior high experience helps broaden the vocabulary. Both children and parents learn the operational meaning of such words as *schedule conflict, priority,* and *choice.* Junior high is that awkward, in-between age when the participants are old enough to be involved but are still too young to provide their own transportation.

Actually, for most young people, junior high represents a time for a much wider assortment of activities, and their involvement does put demands on the family structure.

The Pressure of Participation

As I have stated in previous chapters, variety is characteristic of the age. Junior high people need to experiment and find out what their strengths and interests are. As parents, we have to accept that, despite the inconvenience.

Participation provides a vehicle for some healthy learning experiences. Yet going into junior high is a bit like going into a doughnut store. You simply can't have everything.

Throughout life we are expected to make some choices, and this process of choice is easier for some than others. At the junior high level, the more mature students are usually the more gifted, so they are in heavy demand. All the coaches and directors solicit their participation. On the other hand, the less mature usually have more free time. (Note the paradox. Although the purpose of participation in an activity is to help the young person mature, the already mature people have more and better opportunities to grow.)

No matter how busy your child seems to be, any activities that put him in wholesome contact with other junior highers are important to his development. Yet most parents will quickly notice that participation affects more than the child—it puts demands on the whole family structure.

Refuse to Be Tyrannized

Although I am a strong advocate for parental support of the child's participation, the junior higher is old enough to realize that there are other people in the family. He is also old enough to know that schedules are coordinated days in advance. In other words, I do not think parents have to be tyrannized by their own children.

If your junior higher calls home and says, "Mom, you've got to drop what you are doing and come and take me to play practice because I forgot to tell you," you are not a bad parent if you respond by saying, "No way. You will ride the bus home as we planned. I have had my day planned for a week, and your schedule will just have to fit into mine."

Of course, there will be a little pouting and maybe even a little shouting if your junior higher tends to be bold. But stick to your guns. You have just taught a human being one of the most important lessons he will ever learn. You have taught him that a time schedule is not a matter of life and death, and that other people are as important as he is.

Homework Assignments for Parents

1. What activities has your child begun during the past year? Which ones are likely to be added during the next year? Are both you and he ready to handle the additional involvement?

2. In what ways are your child's extracurricular activities helpful? In what ways do they cause a strain on the family structure? What specific things can you to to maximize the benefits while minimizing the inconveniences?

3. Are you committed to letting your junior higher suffer the consequences if he forgets to let you know about special events in his schedule? In what ways can you make him more responsible without getting him in trouble with teachers, coaches, etc.?

18

When Your Child Learns at a Different Pace

Kathy has a reading problem. It started years ago, perhaps as early as the first grade. Maybe even before. The experts project a lot of guesses about why the Kathys can't read, but they are just guessing. Perhaps she has a physiological problem in the way her brain receives signals from her eyes. Perhaps she never learned her phonics. Or perhaps she just never developed an interest or enthusiasm for reading.

Regardless of the reason, she has a problem. At this point, even though Kathy's reading skills may improve to some extent, so will those of her classmates. Every day the gap gets bigger.

Although Kathy had some difficulty in elementary school, she learned to compensate and managed to keep on top of things. She struggled with schoolwork, but she was active and sociable enough to keep strong friendships with the other girls and to participate in normal elementary school activities. She was a part of the group, and she was generally pleased with herself.

But when Kathy entered junior high, her reading deficiency became a real problem with serious consequences. For one thing, most junior high classwork relies heavily on reading skills. Of course, reading is important for elementary work too, but in junior high most teachers expect the students to read proficiently enough to learn the material through reading.

In other words, there is a greater emphasis on reading as a learning tool. Science teachers, social studies teachers, health teachers, and language arts teachers all expect students to be able to go home and read the chapter for tomorrow's test.

This kind of expectation works against Kathy in two ways. Not only does it take her longer to do the homework, but after all that time, she doesn't get as much out of it as her classmates. Despite her struggling, she still makes lower grades.

Now that Kathy is in junior high, all this has begun to make a difference. If she tries to keep up with her schoolwork, she won't have as much time for social activities. On top of that, she has begun to lose status anyway. Although rank-and-file junior highers don't particularly like the "eggheads" and "teachers' pets," they still put some stock in being successful. So in junior high, there is a stigma attached to the students who struggle academically. Although none of her more capable friends ever make a public announcement of this (in fact, most of them probably don't even know they feel this way), they are gradually and subtly turning away from Kathy.

The Wrong Response for Poor Readers

After watching this happen to dozens of girls over the past twenty-five years, I am inclined to believe that there is an even deeper factor involved here. I am convinced that people at this age perceive reading as a feminine activity. Based on the role models they have observed, they have concluded that reading is a part of womanhood. While men sit home in their undershirts, drink beer, and watch ball games on TV, women curl up in the corner with a good book or a magazine.

So when Kathy reached that age when she came face to face with her reading deficiency and all the subsequent problems, she had to discover another method of self-identity. She chose to try toughness, a fairly common response for junior high girls with reading problems.

Early in her junior high career, she started associating with a tougher crowd than she had been used to. Although these are not bad kids, they are outside the mainstream of things and try to get attention through techniques designed to shock both their classmates and adults. They try to look and act grown-up. Their dress reflects this rebellion. They congregate in the vacant lot across the street where many of them smoke, knowing they are safe from school law.

In class, these students are usually quiet or surly. Since many of them can't read, school isn't much fun. Imagine the tedium of spending most of your day being forced to do something you don't do well. Small wonder they lose interest.

They are very likely to misbehave in class for several reasons, and I don't propose to know all of them. But two main reasons seem common. First, some of these people get so frustrated with their situation that they have to rebel. And second, some of them act up to protect themselves. A person's ignorance is a very precious and private commodity. (I confess to going to great lengths to hide my incompetence from anyone I don't respect.)

So I am not all that surprised when Kathy makes a real scene on the day we are having students read play parts. She simply doesn't see any need to parade her deficiency out for everyone to see. She can't read—she knows that—but there is no need to show it to the rest of the class. So she misbehaves—talking to her friends, practicing her cosmetic skills, or arguing with the teacher. We all get the idea that Kathy is a troublemaker, when all she is doing is what I do every day—camouflaging inadequacy.

A Better Response for Poor Readers

I don't think we can hope for much success treating the symptom until we get to the disease, and helping a child catch up in reading is a difficult task. But in most cases it can be accomplished. At least it is worth a try.

If your child is experimenting with some unusual forms of social compensation, it is probably worth your time and money to get an accurate appraisal of her reading ability. Before bitterness creates a chasm between the two of you, let your child know that you are interested in doing whatever needs to be done to help her.

If your school counselor can't administer the appropriate tests, ask for a recommendation of a professional tester. If you discover a problem, get help. There are several ways to go about this, but the beginning for all of them is to solicit your child's cooperation and goodwill.

You can also help by creating a conducive environment and motivation to read at home, even if it means turning off the TV. Many junior high schools have solid remedial reading programs, and thousands of students are helped through them. But school programs do have some limitations. For one thing, they are not complete within themselves. If your child is going to improve her reading, she is going to have to practice outside school.

If a poor reader has a talent (such as music), be rather insistent in encouraging participation. Success in any area will help fortify the student against the embarrassment of being in the special class. Far too often, special reading programs carry a stigma. The perception is that nice children read well, but the tough ones don't. Often there is a self-fulfilling prophecy. The people in the special reading programs tend to be the toughest kids in school. If your child is assigned to such a class, you should be alert to this possibility. You may need to take some action to counteract it.

Perhaps you're thinking, "I want to know how to live with my teenager at home—let the

teachers worry about her academic problems."
But reading problems will penetrate into *every*
area of life. If the two of you are going to survive
these years, you need to address the issue.

The Plight of Being Bright

But don't assume that good reading skills
will automatically ensure smooth sailing for your
junior higher. Problems exist at the other extreme
as well.

One time while visiting an eighth grade class,
I noticed Richard as soon as I walked in. He was
lean and intense and wore horn-rimmed glasses.
As soon as I could, I worked my way around to
see if I could discover what lurked behind those
horn rims. I decided to check on his reading
material as an opener.

"Is that a science fiction book you are
reading?"

"Yes, it is."

"You must like science fiction." (It was a
lucky guess. Horn-rimmed eighth graders usually
like science fiction.)

"Well, actually, I prefer fantasy."

"Oh, anything in particular?" I had passed
curiosity and was getting in over my head. This
fact-finding tour had just turned educational.

"J. R. R. Tolkien is my favorite. I just finished
the Trilogy and found it totally delightful."

At this point, the girl sitting next to Richard
ventured her opinion of our conversation. "Oh,
shut up," she said convincingly and disgustedly.

Richard reached under the desk, kicked her soundly, and went back to the world of Ray Bradbury and imagination.

Richard is a fun person. Having him in class is a bit of a test, because he sometimes wants to make big deals out of minor points—those points his colleagues fail to remember. He does enhance the discussion, and he challenges the adults around him. But at the same time, Richard's junior high life is not always rosy.

Jessica, described in Chapter 4, matured physically before her time. Richard is simply more mature intellectually than others his age. Where Jessica had an adult body struggling against a child's emotions, Richard has an adult mind struggling against a child's emotions. Jessica had a problem winning acceptance because she *looked* too adult. But Richard has trouble gaining acceptance because he just can't keep from *sounding* adult, at least to the other eighth graders.

Actually, Richard's classmates have an interesting love-hate relationship with him. They tend not to like him too much, particularly when he sounds so pompous, but they don't mind having him around when they need help with their homework. Of course, the low-motivated students don't find him acceptable at all. They either ignore him or ridicule him, but Richard is smart enough to stay clear of them as much as possible.

As intellectuals go, Richard is actually in better shape than some. In addition to being intelligent, he is also gregarious enough not to be ashamed of the fact. It doesn't seem to bother him that he knows the answer when no one else does. He delights in being able to share his knowledge with any prospective listener.

(Think what life must be like for the junior higher who is not only intelligent, but also shy. That poor child is destined to spend some lonely moments before he reaches an age when knowledge and wisdom count for something.)

Stepping Up the Pace

Despite all the appearance of self-sufficiency, Richard and his fellow intellectuals may need more adult understanding and association than some other junior highers. If you have a Richard at your house, his junior high years may be fun for you, but you do need to realize his specific adjustment problems. There are actually two goals here.

First, *we need to provide all Richards with enough encouragement and stimulation to help them keep developing their minds.* School may not provide an adequate challenge. I don't mean to shock anybody with that statement, but educators know it is true. In recent years, some junior high schools have been rather creative in adding programs to encourage the "gifted"—the better-than-average students. But these programs are still not going to meet all of Richard's needs.

After all, it isn't much fun to read Tolkien's Trilogy unless you can discuss it with someone. Richard needs another developed mind to help him satisfy his curiosity and make him feel good about his natural assets.

One way to help him through is to make sure that he is included in some adult discussions, and Richard would probably be willing. If you and your adult friends do not discuss the things that interest Richard, you may have to make a special effort to find him discussion friends. You may need to get him into a special study program or library group.

Of course, there is a hazard. Although Richard reads and, in some ways, thinks like an adult, he is still emotionally thirteen or fourteen years old. This is a problem in selecting reading material as well. Some great literary works are to be read with the intellect. Others are to be read with the emotions, and Richard is still not grown-up emotionally.

This leads to our second goal: *We should make sure that our Richards aren't lonelier than they need to be.* The interesting paradox with Richard is that while he needs some intellectually mature stimuli, he also needs the activities of a junior higher. So you may find yourself taking Richard to the library's great books discussion one evening and to a roller-skating party the next. Isn't it fun!

It would be so much more convenient if all junior highers learned at the same pace, but it's obvious that they don't. So as parents, we need to keep a watchful eye over the progress of our children. If they are a little behind the pack, we may need to encourage them and keep nudging them forward. If they are way ahead, we need to make sure we are there with them to provide companionship and direction. And for all the others who are somewhere in between, someone needs to continually evaluate their progress and apply a proper intensity of motivation. I'll leave that to you.

Homework Assignments for Parents

1. At what pace does your child learn in each of his subjects? (A good reader can be slow in math, for example.) If your junior higher is a little behind the rest of the students, what are you doing to help him catch up? If he is ahead, what are you doing to keep him motivated?

2. As you observe your child's behavior, can any of his actions be attributed to his pace of learning? Do you need to investigate the reason your child is behaving in certain ways?

3. If you are trying to challenge your child intellectually, what are some things you can do to make sure not to rush him emotionally?

19

Learning about Spiritual Things

It's Sunday evening, late July. The church is almost packed on this special night. The junior high youth group has been gone all week to that fun-filled, spiritually significant event which in the good old days we would have called Junior High Camp. But in this age of flashing lights, sound bytes, and electronic music, such a generic name for a spiritual emphasis week won't work. We have to find something fancy, something distinctive, something with style. (You just can't get a bunch of young adolescents excited about an experience as important as camp by calling it *camp*.)

For a while, we used the concept of *retreat*, but the word sounded too passive to describe what really went on during that week. So we tried the word *advance*. That was a step in the right direction, but not quite far enough. Now our junior highers spend their week of spiritual discovery at events identified by far more descriptive names, such as: EXPLOSION, BURST,

TOGETHER, DISCOVERY, ADVENTURE, HIGH ROAD, or AWAKENING.

But whatever this one was called, the junior highers had come home this morning—all twenty-seven of them, exhausted and exhilarated. Now, during the Sunday evening service, they are ready to share their glorious week, their growth, and the meaning of themselves with the entire church family.

This is a big event for the young people involved. For some of them, this will be the first time they have ever spoken (or even been seen) at the front of the church. Some have prepared "official" speeches. Others who will present rather meaningful sermons tonight really haven't planned to say anything, not even on this very special night reserved for this specific purpose. They are the people who have always maintained that, "I would just die if I ever had to stand up and speak in church."

Unlike other Sunday evening services which begin rather slowly and build throughout, the excitement and meaning of tonight's service begins early, with the processional rally. It is a grand entry of spontaneous formality.

First the junior highers gather outside as a group, mostly to give themselves support, but also to share their nervous energy with others just as nervous. Then, as a group, they move forward to take the places reserved for them in the front pews. There is something unique about their stride, something hesitant in their positiveness, something underneath the seriousness which could erupt into uncontrolled giggling in an instant. All of this is part of the significance of the service tonight, and needs to be noticed and marked.

As soon as they take their seats, one bold young fellow toward the center of the group pulls out an old, beat-up cap and dons it with a certain ceremonial flair. Obviously this cap has some kind of special meaning to the group. As one, they laugh appreciatively at his action, and the laughter relaxes them and gives them unity. This too has meaning. That young man's cap has a special story behind it that will have a lasting impression to the members of the group—but only to them.

We who sit around them and watch all this happen may never know its meaning. It is something these young people share together, but they may choose never to let the rest of us in on it. That's all right. I suspect it may be a rather subtle attempt to get back at us for all those times we gave special meaning to events in our worship services which *they* didn't quite comprehend.

After the songs, the offering, and the announcements, we get to the special part of the service—the camp report, or the testimonies, or whatever word we use to label the observations of these young people during the previous week.

We have the prepared speeches first, three guys and two girls. In between the descriptions of "wonderful," "fabulous," and "terrific," we piece together the events of the week—the cookouts, the food fights, the late-night campfire, the all-night conversations in the bunkhouse, the laughter, and the tears. And oh yes, the worship service where some guy preached these neat sermons and we sang these fabulous songs.

After the prepared speeches, we get to the spontaneous ones. The person in charge begins innocently enough by asking, "Does anyone else have anything to say?" He grins at the group. During the following snickers and silence, individuals scrunch further down in their seats so as not to be conspicuous. But about the time we are satisfied that no one else will venture to speak, the fellow with the cap stands in a half-slouch which apologizes even before he opens his mouth.

He says, "I'm not much of a speech maker, but. . . ." (At this point, he remembers the cap, rips it off his head, and begins a sermon from the heart.) "I'm really not a part of this group. Shucks, there were some that I didn't even know their names. But during this week, it was just like a miracle that we all came together and became one giant family. Everybody liked everybody and there weren't any fights. And I've never felt like this before, like, well, I want to feel this way the rest of my life and I love you people and I. . . ."

The sermon goes on and is accepted by the group with the proper combination of giggling and tears. When this fellow has finished and reapplied the cap, others follow with the same kind of message. This week has been a great time for them because they have gotten to know people. They have also learned to like people they haven't liked before. They have forgiven and been forgiven. They have never felt this way before. Some even recall Bible verses which seem significant at the moment.

Spiritual Observations

Now, as adults, let's stop for a moment and do some tough work. Let's analyze what we have just witnessed on this special night. As parents and church youth workers, we often cry out that we just don't understand junior high students. We have no idea what is going on in their minds. Most of them seem to hate church.

For many adults, surrendering to teach the Seventh Grade Boys Sunday School Class is about like David volunteering to go up against Goliath. The only way you can possibly succeed is through a miracle from God. How can we ever tell what is happening to junior highers spiritually during this crucial time in their growth?

Well, I don't propose that we can ever know totally what is going on in a student's relationship with God, just as we never really have that knowledge about anybody. But if we observe carefully and note the right cues, we *can* get an understanding of what a religious commitment means to the group as a whole.

Perhaps we can also understand a little better what is going on in the heart and soul of the individual. For this special understanding, let's notice two common themes during that night of camp debriefing.

Emphasis on Relationships

First, let's take special note of how much *talk centers around relationships*—human relationships and the feelings which grow out of them. There are two characteristics of the junior higher at work here.

For one thing, we need to remember that he is a concrete thinker. He has a hard time wrapping his mind around abstract concepts and principles. We talk of an omnipotent God who directs our ways and gives us abundant life, but the junior higher wants to see the evidence. He wants to know how being a Christian makes him any different from other people. And on a very concrete level, he wants to see the evidence of God at work in *our* lives as adults—in the way we feel, in our actions, and in our relationships with other people.

Let's pause here and state emphatically a very powerful truth. For the most part, the junior high student is going to learn his religion from models. He is going to observe, analyze, compare, and then make decisions. You could probably argue that everybody learns their most important lessons from models, but this is especially true for junior highers who rely so heavily on concrete thinking and resist abstractions so adamantly.

If we are at all interested in their spiritual growth, we must provide our junior-high children with real life examples to guide their pilgrimage. Never in their lives will they look more critically at the relationship between what we *say* we believe and what we *show* we believe. Of course, having the right family models is only a starting point, and there is a good possibility that family models alone won't be enough.

Many junior highers go through a stage when they look upon family members (moms and dads) with a little apprehension. They are simply too close to be objective about what they see, so they search outside the family for the right model. For many, that job falls to the Junior High Sunday School teacher.

The character of people who teach junior highers is more important than what they teach. In fact, the youth worker assigned to the junior high group may well be the most important member of the church structure. I was once a member of a church staff where a Junior High Sunday school teacher was convicted of embezzlement. It took some of those young people twenty years to overcome the bitterness of that lesson.

So what are the requirements to be a spiritual model for people this age? The same as we have discussed in all the other chapters—fairness, consistency, approachability, and genuineness. It's easy to accuse junior highers of not being good listeners. But as a group, they aren't all that impressed with talk in the first place. They primarily want to see what you stand for.

They might cut up, giggle, make fools of themselves, and harass their Sunday school teachers. They may talk and exchange notes in church. But they may also be gathering more spiritual material than we think they are. You can be sure that they are studying their models, and that is the stuff of their spiritual growth.

This demand for concrete models also provides us with a key to their instruction. I have found that junior high students are actually good Bible scholars when we provide them the right material. As concrete thinkers, they are interested in the stories, in the situations, in the people of the Bible and how God related to them, and in the things they can visualize and imagine. Generally they respond well to structure and routines of religious instruction, such as daily Bible readings or performing specific tasks about the church.

Junior highers aren't too interested in studying abstractions they can't grasp or trying to memorize concepts without meaning. I spent twenty years trying to persuade junior high boys that they should memorize 2 Corinthians 5:20: "Now then we are ambassadors for Christ." One day I realized that my students didn't even know what an ambassador was—much less an ambassador for Christ. I had to admit that it is a tough concept which I am not sure I fully understand. In theory, I might have taught a few of those boys something important. But in fact, I taught a lot of them the hidden lesson that religion is too deep for them to grasp.

As our church's junior highers talked of their relationships and their good feelings during the special service, they revealed another characteristic about themselves. They showed the adults

that, to them, the concrete evidence that everything is right in the world is found within the
area of relationships.

When I get all the bills paid or meet a
deadline or get the dishes washed and the kitchen
cleaned, then I get the idea that things are going
fairly well for me. I feel good about myself and I
can focus on more noble thoughts. But the
average junior higher doesn't have all those
outlets for self-identity. About the only satis-
faction he can recognize is within a human
relationship.

So when those relationships are going well,
he senses some success in life and begins to feel
good about himself. A church camp experience
can provide that kind of success in relationships,
so the young person feels better about himself
and somehow connects that positive feeling to
his relationship with God. We may want to
dispute this theologically, but we still sing,
"They'll know we are Christians by our love."

The Great Spiritual Cover-up

After looking at the junior highers'
emphasis on relationships, we also need to take
special note of the *silliness lying just underneath the
seriousness* during that special service. Is it possible
that these people can be thinking about God in
any real way when they are likely to break out in
giggles at the drop of the cap? Of course they can.
Our religious experience is the deepest, most
private part of our very existence.

At times, I have been rather glib when talking of spiritual things. That's because I am still choosy about whom I let into the private part of my being, into my own personal Holy of Holies, into the place where I go to worship. My relationship with God is *mine*.

To the junior higher, vulnerability doesn't come naturally. He lives in fear of being misunderstood, contradicted, or betrayed by himself as well as others. He has to keep up the facade at all times. He has to be very cautious about whom he lets into his inner being and how far he lets them enter. Perhaps the problem is that he doesn't even know himself well enough, and he is still afraid of his own emotions and thoughts. But for whatever reason, he has to stay on guard. And for protection, he uses silliness.

This is common for junior high students in the religious environment, and may account for why they seem so inattentive and distracted in Sunday school or church services. They may be just trying to protect themselves—from themselves as much as from other people. There is a big difference between what they reveal about themselves and what they really think. When you talk to a junior higher by himself, you will usually get a different picture than when you listen to that same person philosophize in a crowd.

I don't understand all the reasoning behind junior high behavior when it comes to spiritual things. Yet from what I can see, I take hope. Let's not underestimate that young guy in the old cap. He may be quite a spiritually mature person.

Homework Assignments for Parents

1. To what extent are you getting involved in your junior higher's spiritual development? Are you demanding certain things, or are you letting him make all his own decisions at this point?

2. Do you recognize your child's spiritual growth and interests, even if he usually hides them behind a "silly" facade? How can you encourage him to be more willing to express his spiritual observations and concerns?

3. At church, do your child's pastor and teachers bring spiritual truths down to concrete levels that can be understood by junior highers? If not, what can you do to help your child translate the abstract lessons into meaningful content?

20

A Closing Check List for Parents

The theme of this book has been that the junior high years are a time of transition for both the child and the parent. The child has to learn to handle changing roles, moods, and body. You as parents have to learn to handle the changing child.

To simplify *your* task, I include this checklist for some of the changes you should be prepared to expect in your child. Although your junior higher may not encounter all of these (and he may encounter some not listed), at least this list should help minimize the surprises you are going to face.

Physical Changes

1. *Growth*—At this age, body growth is as unpredictable as a hummingbird in flight. We never know when or how much. One year my eighth grade basketball team traveled to another town where each of my players was between six and

twelve inches taller than his opponent. Four years later some of those same boys played again, but this time the athletes were the same size. A short time can make a big difference.

These unpredictable growth spurts concern everybody involved. For one thing, there is often some physical pain involved. Problems with joints and shin splints, for example, are common among this age-group.

Another problem is awkwardness. When a graceful thirteen-year-old grows six inches in a matter of a few months, he will quite naturally go through some clumsiness before he regains complete control of his arms and legs. Also, trying to keep your child supplied with clothes can be a horrendous task during this growth stage.

2. *Body Hair*—Again, this is unpredictable and becomes something of a symbol of maturity for many junior highers. Much silent comparison takes place at this age. Your child's need to shave may be more emotional than cosmetic.

3. *Voice Changes*—To get from childish cries to adult tones, one has to go through some squeaks and groans. And those unintentional sounds are not always as humorous for the speaker as they are for the listener.

When an eighth-grade boy answers the phone and is mistaken for his mother, he is embarrassed. Perhaps this is one reason why junior highers prefer each other's company. They don't have to explain the vocal ups and downs.

4. *Sexual Development*—With increased sexual power comes increased curiosity. Junior highers have an imperative need for counseling, direction, and understanding.

5. *Skin Problems*—Regardless of precautions, these are almost inevitable, and are a source of frustration and embarrassment. Part of being a parent is knowing when to consult a dermatologist.

Social Changes

1. *Widening Social Circle*—For most young people, junior high offers a variety of social opportunities. For many, this variety comes unexpectedly and often complicates the role of the parents.

2. *Role Changes*—Junior high is filled with surprises. Popular people lose their starring roles, and unknowns often blossom. These changes never come easily for the participants, because they demand that the young person learn a whole new set of emotional responses.

3. *Family Relationships*—During junior high, your child will need his family identification perhaps more than at any other period in his life, although it may seem as if he is denying it. To younger brothers and sisters, he is a hero. To older siblings, he is a nuisance.

4. *Egocentrism*—As Charlie Brown's friends huddle to discuss the movie they have just seen, he

stands outside and wonders what they are saying about him. The junior higher may often get the idea that he is the center of critical conversation, even though he isn't.

Emotional Changes

1. *The Independent/Dependent Paradox*—The junior higher needs adults, but he may not act like it. Most need some external structure although they may express verbal opposition.

2. *Extremes*—For some unexplained reason (or perhaps for several reasons) the junior higher may pass from one emotion to its opposite at any moment. People in his path may not understand why.

3. *Experimentation*—Since the junior higher is almost always adjusting to something new— voice, body, social role, or whatever—he has to develop a whole new system of emotional responses. This takes some trial and error (and some extreme reactions at times).

Intellectual Changes

1. *Concrete to Abstract*—Developmental psychologists tell us that people should move from thinking in concrete, material terms to more abstract thinking between the ages of twelve to fifteen. This change does not come without

problems. The junior higher has a great need for consistent, concrete models who will demonstrate abstract realities by concrete actions.

2. *Demand for Learning Tools*—During most of elementary school, students work at developing the basic learning skills of reading, writing, and arithmetic functions. In junior high, they are expected to use those skills to master content. If a junior higher is deficient in any skill, he will suffer academically and perhaps socially.

In closing, let me reiterate one point I made early in this book. As painful as it may be, try to remember what *your* life was like during junior high. If you can recall some of the pain, embarrassment, and emotional turmoil you felt, you will vastly improve your ability to help your child through his or her junior high ordeal. I think if you do, you'll discover that any discomfort you feel will be well worth it.

How the Junior High School System Operates

This book has dealt with the confusion faced by junior highers as they undergo drastic changes. Parents of junior highers face uneasy, turbulent times as well. But if it's any consolation, other people are just as confused as you are. In fact, even the educators and psychologists—the people who are supposed to know what this age is all about—sometime seem a little mixed up themselves.

School: How to Name It—And Why

The whole business of training and certifying junior high teachers is just one example. Although teacher certification varies some from state to state, there are enough similarities for us to make an observation. I will use Illinois as an example.

In Illinois, we have two kinds of teachers—elementary and secondary. Elementary teachers prepare themselves in college by spending a large portion of their time studying how to teach methodology. They study how people learn to read, write, and do arithmetic.

It is assumed that these people have a sufficient grasp of the subject matter of elementary grades. To prepare themselves to teach, they need to work on understanding the child and how he learns.

On the other hand, the secondary teachers spend most of their time studying the content of the field they will be teaching. They major in things like history or English or math, and they take a few courses in teaching theory and methodology. It is assumed that they first must know their subject matter; then they can easily learn a few tricks, and they are ready for the next forty years in the classroom.

When the elementary people finish their preparation, they receive a state certificate that affirms their competence to teach grades kindergarten through nine. When the secondary people finish their preparation, their state certificate affirms their competence to teach grades six through twelve.

Now, look at what that says. We really don't know who is supposed to teach grades six through nine! We don't know whether we should turn the education of this critical age-group over to elementary teachers specializing in methodology, or to secondary teachers specializing in content. Or maybe we should give those students a smattering of both.

In all fairness, some colleges (and even some states) have taken the matter more seriously and are now offering a special preparation program for the prospective middle-school teachers. Nevertheless, most students in this age-group are taught by teachers who have not been especially trained for this specific duty.

A real paradox exists here. The basic assumption of this whole book is at stake. I propose that the period of early adolescence is one of the most unusual and most critical periods in a person's development, and wise parents will spend some time preparing themselves especially for the task. Yet educators themselves can't decide whether people at this stage of their lives are at the top end of childhood and should be taught like children or at the bottom end of adulthood and should be taught like adults.

Junior High

During the period from approximately 1835 to 1875, most American children (at least the ones who had the privilege) attended the town's school, which housed grades one through eight. In the history of American education, this period is called the common-school movement.

In 1874, the Supreme Court ruled that Americans could tax themselves to support public high schools. Thus, a whole new school level, the high school, was created. Students who graduated from eighth grade went to another building for grades nine through twelve.

In the early 1900s, some schools decided to experiment with this structure. They pulled grades seven and eight out of the elementary school and grade nine out of the high school and combined them into something they called the junior high school.

The theory seemed workable from a social and educational point of view. Ninth graders were too young to be in the same building with seniors. Seventh and eighth graders were too mature to be in the same building with all the younger children. The junior high school seemed to be a good solution to several problems.

Educationally, these schools basically tried to live up to their name. In other words, they attempted to be "junior" versions of high schools. They attempted to offer watered-down versions of high school courses taught with much the same structure as in high school.

Math teachers taught math, science teachers taught science, and students went from teacher to teacher for an hour a day of specialized study. (This is called *departmentalization* and is to be contrasted with a self-contained classroom where the students are with one teacher for the whole day.)

Although there were some variations, this structure was dominant for the next fifty years or so. But during the sixties when experimentation was in vogue, some educators focused their attention on the early adolescent and came up with something called the middle school.

Middle School

Although the middle school in its purest form is a rather elaborate theory of education, the movement grew out of concern for social compatibility within junior high schools. The big difference between the maturity levels of seventh graders and ninth graders is immediately evident. So the educators reasoned that ninth graders shouldn't be in the same building with seventh graders.

Seventh graders don't need that kind of influence, and ninth graders need more of a social challenge. In many school districts, ninth graders were pulled out of the junior high and placed in the high schools. Then, to make the middle school a three-grade enterprise, the sixth graders were brought up from the elementary schools to be with the seventh and eighth graders.

Presently, the jury is still out concerning the feasibility of this plan. Perhaps the maturity gap between sixth graders and eighth graders is actually greater than the gap between seventh graders and ninth graders. Perhaps the preferable solution would be to have a separate school for each grade level during these years characterized by quick change and extremes. Regardless of the most desirable format educationally, economics will rule out some of my proposals.

Of course, the middle-school engineers and advocates contributed more than a new social structure. They reasoned that the unique people in this age-group also needed a unique school experience, one which provided for the students' basic needs: freedom and structure, transition from childhood into adolescence, experimentation, and educational review.

The middle school, then, in its original form, attempted to provide for these needs. Consequently, a large share of the educational experimentation and innovation in the last twenty years has been directed toward the grades six through nine.

Despite the continuing confusion about preparation and certification of teachers, educators are still trying to get it right. Just to know that even the educators are working on the problem should be some comfort to parents who are concerned that they don't understand their own child as well as they would like.

To get a closer study of some of these educational theories at work presently, let's look in on three different teachers, each representing a different approach to educating the junior higher.

Classroom Innovator

Ralph Cowper teaches "eighth-grade core." That isn't a class in apple appreciation; it's a combination of English and social studies. Mr. Cowper's school is generally departmentalized. In other words, the day is divided into seven periods, and the students pass from class to class for most of their studies. But there is that nagging notion that students this age need a bit more stability. They need some deeper identification with a specific teacher, and they need the opportunity to be with one social group for a greater length of time.

So in Mr. Cowper's school, that need for stability is met by combining English and social studies into core class, which meets for two periods. The class provides the students with something of a homeroom. They are with their classmates for a block of time. Since the core teachers have only three sections per day, they have an opportunity to get better acquainted with the individual students.

Mr. Cowper himself is an interesting teacher. He is highly educated—having studied overseas in some prestigious programs. He is active in social studies circles and has published papers in history journals. In the evenings, he teaches specialized courses for one of the local colleges. But Mr. Cowper is a confirmed junior high teacher. He spends most of his time with junior high students. He not only teaches them in the classroom and prepares for his classes at night, but he also supports the junior high activities.

He attends the sports events and musical presentations. He invites junior highers into his home. He counsels with them during lunch and throughout the day. During passing periods, he stands outside his door and calls most of the students by name. Because he is so interested in them and because they know he is interested in them, he has earned the right to discipline any student at school. So when a students runs in the hall, Mr. Cowper handles the situation.

WHAT PARENTS TRY TO FORGET

In simple terms, Mr. Cowper is a junior high teacher, and he doesn't want to be anything else. He has no false notion of himself as a high school teacher or a college history professor. He understands how junior highers learn, and he likes to teach these people who have some special learning and social needs.

Mr. Cowper's classes are characterized by direction and flexibility. He provides the students with a sense of direction by such little considerations as putting the daily objectives and assignments on the chalkboard. When the students walk into the room, they glance at the board and know immediately what they are to do that day and what is expected of them. Since they know what must be learned, there is always a bit of urgency about the class, a feeling that the class must move forward because there are important things ahead.

At the same time, Mr. Cowper's scheduling allows for flexibility. This is one of the advantages of the two-hour period. If during a discussion about one topic, some student asks a meaningful question about another topic, Mr. Cowper may have the students gather into a circle and discuss that related topic before they go on with the rest of the lesson.

Or if a side topic seems important to a couple of students, Mr. Cowper may assign them a bit of extra research; and when they have finished, he gives them the opportunity to report to the class. In his class, students have an opportunity to pursue things that really interest them.

Mr. Cowper does utilize small groups frequently. He also uses such teaching techniques as role playing and simulations. In his simulations, the students take a role in a semi-real situation, and they play that role for a while. In fact, one of the major learning experiences of the year is the Model Congress where the students simulate national Congress and play their roles until they have learned how Congress works and laws are passed and implemented.

Since Mr. Cowper knows how a junior high student operates, since he knows about the changes in moods and perspectives, and since he has chosen to teach in junior high, he is not afraid to create situations where the students can feel free to express themselves while they are learning. He gives them frequent opportunities to think, to write, and to present their ideas to class. In other words, he activates the students in the learning process. He accepts their ideas and all their changes. He offers them consistent support through their critical development period. He gives them room to experiment academically, but he also provides enough direction to keep them in bounds.

Obviously, Mr. Cowper is a popular teacher. His former students drop by to see him and thank him for the direction he provided while they were in junior high school. Mr. Cowper also has a supportive administration and administrative policy. The educational theory at his school is that junior high students should be introduced to as many experiences and studies as possible during the seventh and eighth grades. The students in the school take semester-long courses in art, music, drama, shop, and homemaking in addition to their other courses in science and math and the two-course block of core.

Academically, junior high is a period of transition—of transition from the elementary emphasis on learning skills such as reading and writing to high school emphasis on mastering content. Mr. Cowper and his school are providing the students an opportunity to explore themselves, their own minds and abilities, and the world of studies during these transition years.

Straight Lecture

Mr. McCaullay teaches eighth-grade American History. He really didn't mean to, but it was the only job he could get. During his college career, Mr. McCaullay fell in love with history and history teaching. He really got excited about those more informal profs who sat on the edge of their desks and told exciting stories about Civil War battles and heroes with shady personal lives.

Mr. McCaullay decided that he could be happy doing this the rest of his life, so he took the required courses to become a secondary history teacher. When he finished college and couldn't find a position with a high school, he settled for a job with a junior high.

He told me at the time that it really didn't matter that much. After all, junior high students are only smaller versions of high school students.

He could still get excited about making history lectures interesting. He only had to watch out for the big words and cut down on the content a bit. But he could teach eighth grade for a few years, get his feet on the ground, and move into a high school job when one came along.

And now, Mr. McCaullay, in the highest form of praise to his college professors, teaches the eighth graders as he was taught. He sits on the front of his desk and tells interesting tales from the fascinating world of history. His students sit at their desks and practice their skills of listening.

Mr. McCaullay, aware that these young people are not as astute at hearing as his college class was, frequently provides them with some listening aids. He gives them outlines to follow or maps to look at, and he assigns readings in the textbook. Students who are motivated (whatever that means) read the assignments and listen carefully in class. Those who are not so inclined listen as best they can, but remain convinced that video games are more fun.

After he has filled several days with his stories, Mr. McCaullay stops and presents the students with a test to see how much they have heard. Some do well; others don't. Since Mr. McCaullay is a good teacher and is concerned about his students, he provides an opportunity for those who have not done well to redeem themselves with another try or extra-credit work. In the meantime, he goes back to telling history stories because he must get through the book before the end of the year. Besides, his favorite period is World War I, and he doesn't want to shortchange that section.

Mr. McCaullay's students have learned some important lessons. They have learned to come to class with paper and pencil, and they have learned to sit quietly and attentively. Unlike Mr. Cowper, Mr. McCaullay does not have the students do oral presentations. He tried it once, but he found them to be extremely nervous and incapable of presenting a cogent project. Some of his students actually refused to make a presentation and chose an F for the assignment.

Now, before you get the wrong idea, let me assure you that Mr. McCaullay is a nice guy who genuinely cares about his students. In fact, some—those who are reserved and intellectual—consider him the best teacher they have. I am glad that he is in the school. But he does reflect a different attitude and approach to teaching the junior high age.

Mr. McCaullay sees the junior high as a time for students to begin to think and act like high schoolers, so he uses the teaching style most common to high school history teaching. He might actually admit, when cross-examined, that the junior high student is different in some ways. But he isn't too happy with that difference, so he chooses to ignore it. He and his students go on about their daily business of covering history as he waits patiently for a more important job of teaching high school to come along.

It might be interesting to note that standardized tests, those national exams which tell us how many facts students have catalogued in their brains, will probably reveal that Mr. McCaullay's students are learning about as much history as Mr. Cowper's. This isn't really so startling. In fact, a comparison of types of junior high teachers is valuable to us. It demonstrates the junior higher's resilience and ability to adapt.

Same Class, Same Teacher, Same Classmates

Mrs. Smith teaches eighth grade. "Eighth grade what?" you ask. Eighth grade everything! Everything? Yes, everything! Language arts, history, reading, spelling, health, art, drama, music, and even Phys Ed two days a week.

Mrs. Smith teaches what the educators call a self-contained eighth grade. There aren't many of these kinds of classes left. (There aren't too many Mrs. Smiths still around either.) Yet there are enough to justify our looking into the class and the educational and social theories at work here.

Mrs. Smith teaches in an elementary building that houses grades kindergarten through eight. In that building, the sixth, seventh, and eighth grades are treated much like the lower grades. At the beginning of the year, students are assigned to a specific section, room, or teacher, and they stay with that group throughout the year. Mrs. Smith received her thirty students the first day of school, and they spend all day with her except for the hour they go to a math specialist.

Mrs. Smith was trained as an elementary teacher, and for the past twenty-five years she has taught mostly fourth or fifth grade. During the last few years, she has taught eighth grade. She teaches her eighth graders much like she taught her fourth graders, except she uses bigger words and covers more material.

As a veteran teacher, she organizes the school day around a common theme. Each morning, the students begin work on some sort of language arts project—a writing assignment, a short story to read, or a poem to memorize. But then, almost as if in the middle, Mrs. Smith cuts the assignment off and goes on to the social studies lesson. From social studies, the class moves to health, drama, music, and art. Two days a week, as the afternoon begins to wear everyone down, the students push the desks aside and venture into vigorous exercises (square dancing, aerobic movement, or chair tag) to satisfy their need for Phys Ed.

At first glance, a visitor might get the idea that Mrs. Smith's students do not receive as much intensified history study as Mr. McCaullay's students get during that one specialized period with him. However, as common themes keep recurring at odd times, the students probably finish the day with more exposure to the social studies material than they would have had during a single specialized period.

Since Mrs. Smith's thirty students are together all day long, they don't need to build a wide base of acquaintances with a lot of other eighth graders in the school. In Mr. McCaullay's school, his students may be in classes with as many as one hundred different eighth graders during the day. In Mr. Cowper's school, students may have classes with as many as seventy different people. But in Mrs. Smith's classes, these students only need to build friendships with their thirty classmates.

This helps provide them with a great deal of security. After a few days together, the students form a supportive bond. They seem to enjoy each other. They are not afraid of one another. They have more freedom to be themselves. The more timid students tend to be particularly happy with this arrangement. A general feeling of goodwill and cooperation is felt throughout the room.

This peer security is probably most evident in oral presentations and speeches. As you remember, Mr. McCaullay's students were reluctant to stand in front of their classmates, and Mr. Cowper's students made presentations with some confidence. But Mrs. Smith's students are regular hams. When she gives them the opportunity, they jump at the chance. They are not afraid to let their classmates laugh at them.

Since Mrs. Smith has only thirty students, she knows them well. She might admit that she knows some of them *too* well, but she does know them. She knows when babies are born into their families. She knows when their dogs die. She knows which students have fathers. She knows which ones are running around with older students. She knows who has friends and who needs friends. And she just might use this knowledge subtly the next time she has need for small group work for an art project.

Overall, Mrs. Smith's students seem rather happy to be in her class. They don't seem to be in too big a hurry to graduate into that foreign world of high school and departmentalization.

"Why then," you ask, "don't we put all junior highers in self-contained classrooms if they receive so much security and happiness in such an arrangement?" There are two obvious answers. First, some students couldn't stand that much security. They simply need more room and more time. They need the variety of having class with a hundred different people.

But the other answer is even more obvious. Mrs. Smith's class works because Mrs. Smith is an excellent teacher. She makes it work. Students don't naturally come together into a close, cooperative society simply because they are thrown together for most of the day. Mrs. Smith provides the needed engineering.

If those students had a poor teacher, one who didn't care or couldn't get the job done, their self-contained class could be devastating. That's one thing you can say for the system at Mr. McCaullay's school. If a teacher is incompetent, the students only have to tolerate him one hour a day.

What's the Best Teaching System?

I present the descriptions of these three teachers for a couple of reasons. First, I want you to see some of the ways educators are attempting to answer the question, "What do we do with junior highers?" Each of these three teachers is quite competent, but each is operating on different theories regarding the general character of junior highers. Although they all could present a persuasive argument for what they are doing, they are all guessing.

No one knows the best way of dealing with the entire age-group of junior high students. At that age they simply experience too much variety in moods, emotions, needs, and maturity levels. Obviously, there is no single correct way to educate or deal with the junior higher.

The second reason I present these descriptions is to help you get some idea of what is happening to your child at school—the enterprise that takes up about a third of his day. I would like for you to be aware of the kinds of activities he encounters and the various attitudes of the people who exercise authority over him. By seeing his teachers in action, maybe you can get a better idea of how to complement and coordinate his experience so that both of you can live happily during those years when a junior higher invades your home.